MW00592683

YAHOO!®

ultimate guide
to finance and money
on the Web

YAHOO!®

ultimate guide
to finance and money
on the Web

from bonds to bills, mortgages to mutual funds,

credit to car loans

By Julie M. Fenster

A Byron Preiss Book

HarperResource
An Imprint of HarperCollinsPublishers

Dedicated to my parents
who like handwritten letters, magazines on the
mailtray, chat in cafes . . . and asking me to look
things up on the internet for them.

JMF

YAHOO! ULTIMATE GUIDE TO FINANCE AND MONEY ON THE WEB
Copyright © 2000 by Yahoo! Inc., 3420 Central Expressway, Santa Clara 95053

All rights reserved. Yahoo! and all related marks, designs and indicia are trademarks of Yahoo!.
Printed in the United States of America. No part of this book may be used or reproduced in any
manner whatsoever without written permission, except in the case of brief quotations embodied in
critical articles and reviews. For information address HarperCollins Publishers Inc., 10 East 53rd
Street, New York, NY 10022.

HarperCollins books may be purchased for educational, business, or sales promotional use. For information, please write: Special Markets Department, HarperCollins Publishers Inc. 10 East 53rd Street,
10022.

FIRST EDITION

Library of Congress Cataloging-in-Publication Data has been applied for.
ISBN 0-06-105878-5
00 01 02 03 04 10 9 8 7 6 5 4 3 2 1

Contents

PART THREE: Making Money

Introduction

The first five years were the search 'n' surf era for the Web. So many websites, so many places to visit—why, there might be 15 or 20 that touched on any single question! The abundance of this new Internet was a marvel, its generosity irresistible. The latest era, however, is fast losing patience with that very abundance. What was once so thrilling is becoming the problem, which is so often the way. There are too many websites cluttering up the route to the clear answers. Web users of today are even starting to distrust the generosity—perhaps you've noticed the average website promising so much more than it actually delivers.

Perhaps you've noticed, too, though, that a handful of websites in any category provide even more than they promise, overflowing with information, ideas, and opportunities. Those are the ones we selected for this book: the lively sites, rife with updated information. We especially like interactive sites—ones that invite you to do more than just read. Those that can be intelligently customized to not only show you what to think about your finances, but how to think about them. Sites with these characteristics indicate the choices you have and the priorities you should set, and they do so more vividly than any book, talk, or television program could. That's the kind of site we searched out to feature.

If a website is like a single word, standing by itself, then a sentence is bound to be better. This book, the **Yahoo! Ultimate Guide to Finance and Money on the Web**, uses websites in sentences by addressing each question about finance as a multi-step process.

Anyone who is looking for a mutual fund, for example, will

find three steps on our chapter, which map the best route through the Web on that subject. The sites in the first step describe the various categories of mutual funds. Those in the second step hone in on making a specific selection, with recommendations, ratings, and stock-screening tools. The third step in the chapter describes the best sites for keeping up-to-date with your funds: featuring news, trends, and other current information that helps you make sure an investment remains as effective in the future as it was the day it was purchased.

The descriptions of the sites in this book show specifically and clearly how you can make the best use of each. Website descriptions that are vague or general leave more of the work to you, forcing you to go to the site and try to find your way through it. That's not worthwhile. And so we don't merely cite our sites, we include directions for use.

With an array of websites selected so that they fit together like sentences, and descriptions that give you a true recipe for success with each of them, the **Yahoo! Ultimate Guide to Finance and Money on the Web** is a new kind of a book for the next era of the Internet.

Keep in mind as you use your **Ultimate Guide** that you needn't utilize every single site in each of our steps. We included enough sites to allow a choice within each step. One point we do hope you'll notice: we favor classy, well-organized sites. Those garish ones that look like Times Square in the middle of a tornado rarely have much worthwhile information, anyway. Very few will show up in this book: We're pretty sure you prefer sites that keep to their business in an undistracting way.

More important, the sites featured in your **Ultimate Guide** are free, with only a very few exceptions. Therefore, just about all the tools and information needed to research personal finance on the Internet is yours for the asking.

You may also note that for the majority of the sites we have included where the site is headquartered. That goes against the prevailing attitude that Cyberspace is just a great global village (although a beautiful, humanistic thought). However it is the strict advice of the **Yahoo! Ultimate Guide to Finance and Money on the Web** that when it comes to *your* money and *your* finance, you know with whom you are dealing and where they can be found. We practice what we preach, in the hope of pressing that point home.

In the early planning stages for the **Ultimate Guide**, we thought we would concentrate on the investment information for which Yahoo! Finance is the accepted center of the Internet. However, e-commerce is another vital aspect of your money—and so is regular old boulevard commerce. In fact, spending money wisely is the first habit of finance; saving it the second; and investing it only comes third. John D. Rockefeller made the point that it is essential for every person, of any means, to spend money wisely, and so do we, by including chapters that let the Internet show the way to savvy consumerism. As you glance through chapters such as Automobiles, Travel, and Shopping, don't assume that we are telling you what car to drive, where to vacation, or what to buy. (A Bentley convertible, Vermont in the spring, and more copies of this book—respectively. I couldn't resist.) But everything else, you're about to find out by yourself—for yourself.

Yahoo! Finance: like money in the bank

During the development of the Internet, Yahoo! evolved from a navigational guide offering links by the score into something even more: a stand-alone journal of news, data and interactive choices.

Yahoo! Finance, a source for financial news, stock quotes, and other personal finance information, has become an essential tool over the same short time span—recognized by academics, government agencies, traders and professional money managers as the financial center of the Internet. Both extensive and flexible, Yahoo! Finance thrives upon convenience, answering most of your needs in a mere couple of clicks.

In the olden days of four or five years ago, financial research was only for the hardy. You had to stomp around libraries, carrying thick volumes of S&P reports, and looking for old magazines—sometimes, outdated information was only kind available. But that is all in the past: Yahoo! Finance brings all levels of financial research right to hand, leaving no excuse for that bane of all markets (and family fortunes): the ill-informed investor.

In this section, the features of Yahoo! Finance are broken down according to the many types of research you will need as you organize your financial plans. Initially we'll discuss Yahoo! Finance from the point-of-view of investing, focusing

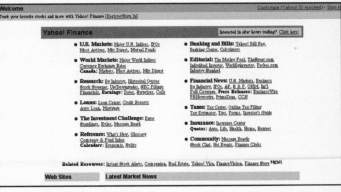

on finding information about markets, stocks, mutual funds and the like. Later we'll cover what we call the home portfolio, including matters of personal finance, such as bill payments, taxes, loans and insurance.

stocks and portfolios: following the market

Some of the most popular features on Yahoo! Finance offer ways to stay abreast of market activity and pricing for any particular stock. Stock Quotes can be found at the top of Yahoo! Finance. Just type in the ticker symbol for any stock or mutual fund and you will see its trading price, as well as other up-to-date information. In fact, you can edit your stock quote pages to include any information you may want, whether it's average trading volume, Price/Earnings ratio, or a chart of the stock price over a certain span of time; you can do this by creating a customized, new View.

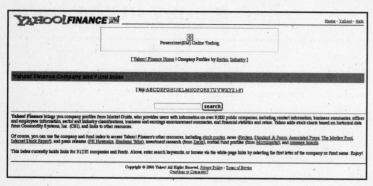

There is another, highly sophisticated way to check your stock quotes at Yahoo! Finance: the Customized Portfolio will not only give you quotes for issues you select, but financial information like the Company earnings as well. At a glance, you can see the worth of the whole portfolio, and even a projection of your annualized return—presuming you maintain the same pace all year. You can customize the way that your portfolio and the quotes within it are presented, choosing from thirty-four different fields to create one View or several, for the fullest understanding of your investment ideas. Likewise, Yahoo! Finance allows you to customize the company news that accompanies your Portfolio. If you want the data to work with your own research tools, Yahoo! Finance Portfolios can be downloaded in spreadsheet formats such as Excel or Quicken. Because you can maintain as many Custom Portfolios as you want, Yahoo! Finance allows you to try out various investment strategies and compare them, before you commit actual money.

For those people who follow individual issues closely, there is extensive company news at Yahoo! Finance. If you are viewing your portfolio, you can reach the News link in the More Info area.. You are likely to find what you need, considering that the site's News content is drawn from such a wide array of sources: *Forbes*, Reuters, S&P, PR Newswire, BizWire, The Motley Fool, *Red Herring, Upside*, CBS MarketWatch, ZDNet, CNet, ON24 (audio and

Yahoo! definition

S&P Reports: Standard & Poor's has been reporting on companies for investors for over a hundred years, supplying both financial data and subjective ratings of share performance

Yahoo! definition

Prospectus: A legal representation of both financial strength and weakness made by any entity seeking outside investors; it is a mandatory publication for mutual funds

video) and Individual Investor, as well as the Associated Press news wire. The News section can be searched by company, industry, or publication to find the news relevant to your investments. If you are in the midst of researching a specific company, you can also find a list of pertinent stories simply by clicking the News button on its Quote page.

A lot of care has been expended by investors over the last century-and-a-half in trying to decide to what extent each stock goes its own way and to what extent groups of them move as one. Indices such as the Nasdaq Composite became popular among people who leaned toward the idea that stocks of a feather move together. Not only do indices allow for comparison of individual stock performance against a sector or market average, they quantify the direction of investor mood, reporting it succinctly as a number. Yahoo! Finance reports throughout the day on more than 25 indices on the U.S. Markets, starting with the Dow Jones Industrial Average. Nothing in finance is as well publicized as the Dow 30, but U.S. Markets also includes every other germane bellwether, such as the S&P 500 and the rather more obscure Philadelphia Semiconductor Index. About 50 indices are kept up-to-date under World Markets on the home page, from the familiar Nikkei 225 of Japan to the Karachi 100 from Pakistan.

The Initial Public Offering (IPO) section of Yahoo! Finance lists recent offerings and ones set to go on sale in the near future. For those whose only interest in IPOs is cashing in on one of those morning-glory issues (one that shoots up in the morning and is old news by the afternoon), Yahoo! Finance charts the best and worst performers over several recent time-spans. Spend twice as much time looking at the "Worst" as at the "Best," and you ought to come to your senses about getting rich quick in IPOs. One recent issue went down 94 percent in its first month.

For many individual investors, mutual funds represent a comfortable way to enter the markets and attain a goal. Yahoo! Finance has a great tool in the Company and Fund Index for researching mutual funds, allowing you to download a prospectus

---

Yahoo! definition

Dow 30: Another name for the Dow Jones Industrial Average, which charts a portfolio containing 30 of America's largest and most respected companies

---

Yahoo! definition

S&P 500: A group of stocks chosen by Standard & Poor's to reflect the most powerful companies in the American economy, the S&P 500 is considered to be representative of the stock market as a whole.

Yahoo! definition

Wilshire 5000: Originated by a firm called Wilshire Associates in Los Angeles, the Wilshire 5000 is an index of every U.S. company traded on the major exchanges (actually, it counts about 7,000 stocks).

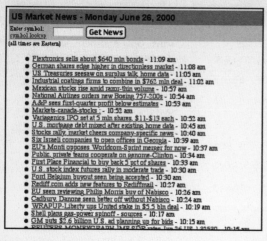

US Market News - Monday June 26, 2000

Enter symbol:
symbol lookup _____ [Get News]
(all times are Eastern)

- Flextronics sells about $640 mln bonds - 11:09 am
- German shares edge higher in directionless market - 11:08 am
- US Treasuries seesaw on surplus talk, home data - 11:05 am
- Industrial coatings firms to combine in $762 mln deal - 11:02 am
- Mexican stocks rise amid razor-thin volume - 10:57 am
- National Airlines orders new Boeing 757-200s - 10:54 am
- A&P sees first-quarter profit below estimates - 10:53 am
- Markets-canada-stocks : - 10:52 am
- Variagenics IPO set at 5 mln shares, $11-$13 each - 10:52 am
- U.S. mortgage debt mixed after existing home data - 10:45 am
- Stocks rally, market cheers company-specific news - 10:40 am
- Six Israeli companies to open offices in Georgia - 10:39 am
- EU's Monti opposes Worldcom-Sprint merger for now - 10:37 am
- Public, private teams cooperate on genome-Clinton - 10:34 am
- First Place Financial to buy back 5 pct of shares - 10:33 am
- U.S. stock index futures rally in moderate trade - 10:30 am
- Ford Belgium buyout seen being accepted - 10:30 am
- Rediff.com adds new features to Rediffmail - 10:27 am
- EU seen reviewing Philip Morris buy of Nabisco - 10:26 am
- Cadbury, Danone seen better off without Nabisco - 10:24 am
- WRAPUP-Liberty ups United stake in $5.5 bln deal - 10:19 am
- Shell plans gas-power spinoff - sources - 10:17 am
- GM puts $2.6 billion U.S. ad planning up for bids - 10:15 am
- REUTERS MONEYGRAPH IMF SDR rates Jun 26 US 1.31520 - 10:15 am

for nearly any one. Other helpful areas for fund research include Profile Overview, Performances, Holdings, and News. However, if you don't yet know what fund to buy . . . then you can join a crowd of several million other people at any one time in this country. With upwards of 8,000 funds listed, Yahoo! Finance's fund selector can winnow the list, with a questionnaire that asks you to fill in about eight fields: One is the number of Morningstar stars you require of a fund. If you fill in "four" or "five" (out of five), the resulting field will have a better chance of representing higher-quality funds.

You have undoubtedly heard time and time again that we are now living in a global marketplace. That's nothing new—it's been a global marketplace for at least a thousand years. However, the markets are indeed moving faster than in the days when people traveled between them in boats with oars. The International Finance Center on the Yahoo! Finance home page comes complete with a tool able to calculate exchange rates between currencies ranging from the Afghan Afghani to the Zambian Kwacha. However, the separate country sites for Yahoo! Finance offer an even closer view of business overseas. One way to use the country sites is to keep track of overseas subsidiaries of any U.S. company in which you have shares. Each of these international sites is directed at residents of the particular country, and so English is not the language used on all of them.

Whether you are just learning to invest or can run circles around J. Paul Getty, you can test your mettle in the Investment Challenge. Part simulation, part competition, it is a monthly game that gives you a portfolio of $100,000 in (virtual) cash with which to take positions in the markets. The players with the most money in their accounts on the last day of the month earn prizes in real money, with $5,000 for the first-place finisher.

Yahoo! definition

National Credit Agencies: Three national companies— Experian, Trans-Union and Equifax—maintain files on Americans, their spending habits, and their use of credit.

companies and funds

For more information on companies and mutual funds, Yahoo! Finance has the Company and Fund Index. This tool would be fairly remarkable even if it covered only a selection of big companies: the Dow 30, for example, or even the S&P 500. It would be a boon if it covered every company in the Wilshire 5000, but the fact is that the index offers detailed information on over 30,000 companies and funds. Located most easily under the heading of Reference on the Yahoo! Finance home page, it is the place to begin perusing any shareholding investment. Type in the name of a company and five categories of information are offered: Quote, Profile, Research, Messages, and Insider.

If you're just getting to know the company, look first under Profile: It starts out in plain English, describing exactly what the company does to make money. These descriptions are usually taken directly from SEC filings and are legally accurate, with no wishful thinking allowed. In addition, the Profile lists company officers and their salaries. Look up almost any well-known stock to see what the bigwigs are making. Along the left side of the page, the Profile offers links to lists of the top institutional shareholders and the top mutual fund shareholders, so that you can gauge the type of investors who are attracted to the company . . . and those that hold influence over it. Of equal interest, the Profile page lists the percentage of outstanding shares held by those within the company. While this figure is typically higher for younger companies, it can nonetheless be an indication of the sheer torque of company growth.

You probably don't need to be told that General Motors competes with Ford in the car business, but it may be enlightening to see GM's competition in less well-known parts of its business, such as communication and financial services. Under Competitors, click on each link for a list of the company competitors by industry sector. Rounding out the background research is a page called Journal Archives, providing a list of recent articles about the company in question. Most of the citations include abstracts: one-paragraph summaries of the material in the article. For financial data, the Pro-

> **Yahoo! definition**
>
> **Indices (or indexes):** An index is a group of stocks generally used as a representative sample of a much larger group of stocks; following their combined performance can help highlight overall trends.

> **Yahoo! definition**
>
> **Fixed-rate:** In a fixed-rate loan, the same percentage is charged in interest throughout the life of the loan.

file page contains quite a bit, as well as offering a direct link to the company's SEC filings.

The Profile page of Yahoo! Finance's Company and Fund Index also provides a well-rounded introduction to a company, whether you mean to work for it, sell to it, buy from it, or simply acquaint yourself with it. However, the Research page looks at the company (or fund) specifically as an investment. Yahoo! details the number and direction of broker recommendations concerning the stock, its earnings, and estimates surrounding that figure. These figures can serve to apprise you of the perception of the stock in the markets, and of its vigor, purely as a money-making enterprise.

Finally, with the benefit of all of this material, you can click on Quote and begin to consider buying shares of attractive companies. But hold off until after downloading and reading the prospectus (for mutual funds) or the company report, along with all or most of the articles collected about the company on the site's news file. Then you will be about as ready as Yahoo! Finance can make you to begin making money in the stock market.

message boards and clubs

The most spontaneous feature of Yahoo! Finance may be the one written entirely by visitors to the site: the Message Boards. Each board covers a particular investment subject or company through an on-going question, answer and comment session. Easy to read and, after a simple e-mail verification process, easy to post a message or question, these boards are a good way to see what people are talking about. They are conveniently found by clicking on the Msgs link in the More Info area of a quote or portfolio.

For those interested in a more structured Internet community, Yahoo! Finance hosts thousands of clubs, each with its own news, members, and, of course, on-going chat. Like the Message Boards, the clubs can pertain to specific companies or business topics and a few of the more popular are run by business schools. If you don't see a club you'd like among the thousands already in place, it is easy to set one up and collect new members. A club can either be public or private, with access only for those you invite to participate. You can get to the Net Events calendar through the Community

Balloon Loan: In a balloon loan, the payments are scheduled to be quite low for a set number of years and then expand into a relatively enormous final payment to complete the purchase.

section of the Yahoo! Finance home page.

If you are interested in still more talk at Yahoo! Finance, the site sponsors a wide variety of Net Events, including live chats with business figures. They are listed on a calendar, so that you can plan you day or week to intersect with any Net Event of special interest.

home portfolio
bill pay

The system behind Yahoo! Finance Bill Pay is as straight-forward as any you might have devised for the once-a-month sit down at the kitchen table at home—except that it is quite a lot neater with no stamps, checks or envelopes required. You designate the amount of each payment, along with when and where it should be sent. For recurring payments, like your rent or cable TV bill, set it up once and have a payment sent out every month automatically. Or set up reminders for other bills so you're never late again. To learn more, you can take a tour of Yahoo! Bill Pay and see it step by step. In most cases, the charge for the Bill Pay service will be between two and seven dollars per month, depending on the plan you choose and the number of bills you pay.

banking center

The Banking Center offers you access to accounts —your accounts, that is—at a growing number of banks worldwide. If you are in the process of choosing an online bank, the site also carries ratings of over a dozen institutions. To help you gauge choices in savings or in loans, the Banking Center lists current national average rates in a variety of banking categories, from CD's to mortgages.

tax center

To cut your taxes for next year, here is a simple tip: Just read the tax prep checklist at the Tax Center on Yahoo! Finance. It lists the records you'll need to save during the tax year to optimize your filing. The checklist, like all smart tax tips, is 90 percent planning—and keep in mind that by April, the opportunity for planning is practically gone. The Tax Center offers a whole library of tax tips, which you should scan for changes each year. Also worth looking at

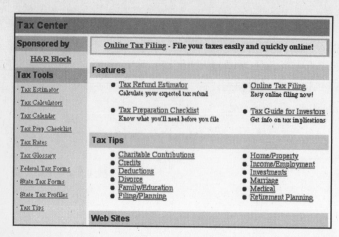

periodically during the tax year is the calendar of IRS dates and deadlines. While you can download state and Federal tax forms that can be printed out and mailed, the Yahoo! Finance Tax Center also offers an e-filing service for a small fee. One of my favorite sections of the Center is the articles on tax information for investors, prepared in association with Fairmark Press.

insurance center

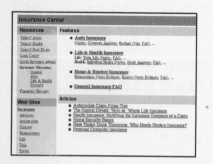

You need insurance to protect so much in your life: your car, your home and belongings, and most importantly, your health and the well-being of your loved ones. The Insurance Center on Yahoo! Finance helps you to understand the choices you need to make: How much coverage do you need? Should you have a lower deductible or a higher premium? Should you choose an HMO (Health Maintenance Organization) or a PPO (Preferred Provider Organization) for your health care? With answers to frequently asked questions like these as well as detailed glossaries, calculators and questionnaires, the Insurance Center helps you make your own evaluation of your insurance needs. And when you are ready, you can apply for a policy directly online.

loan center

One of the awkward aspects of applying for a loan is ascertaining, as quietly as possible, whether or not you have a realistic chance of receiving the amount requested. Each of the three sections in the Loan Center at Yahoo! Finance's—home mortgage, auto, and small business—start with "quick estimates," to let you know the charges and payments you can expect in any loan described. The mortgage center follows with another short questionnaire, designed to identify the most suitable type of mortgage for you. As you probably know, the choice these days is abundant, and overall costs can be whittled away substantially by finding the right type of mortgage: seven-year balloon, five-year fixed-rate and so forth. Other questionnaires on the site can help you to make a decision about refinancing, or to make the basic choice between renting and buying. The automobile loan center can supply rates for either new or used vehicles, according to your state and driving record. It follows with over a dozen calculators, which help highlight the decision points along the way in the process of auto finance. Yahoo! Finance also offers quotes on several types of small business loans, including general purpose loans; commercial and equipment financing; and Small Business Administration-sponsored loans.

If you are applying for a loan, it behooves you to see your credit report. The loan officer certainly will see it, and you ought to know what is in it. Yahoo! Finance has two different services: For $7.95, you can see your report online; for $29.95, you will receive by post a merged report, containing information from all three national credit agencies. At no cost, you can have your credit analyzed, giving you a general indication of your credit-worthiness. All that is needed are the answers to about a dozen questions, mostly pertaining to your use of credit cards. The Analyzer will then give you a rating ranging from one to five stars, with a short explanation. Think carefully about your answers to the questions: they indicate the concerns of credit bureaus and are good to keep in mind.

Loan Center

Resources	Features
· Yahoo! Finance	● **Mortgage Center**
· Insurance Center	Mortgage Quotes, Recommendations, Rates...
· Financial Glossary	
· Credit Report	● **Auto Loan Center**
· Local Lenders	Auto Loan Quotes, Calculators, Rates...
· Yahoo! Real Estate	
· Yahoo! Autos	● **Small Business Loans**
· Yahoo! Small Business	
· Yahoo! Visa	● **Credit Reports**

Web Sites	Articles
· Financing	● Mortgages: Understanding the Loan Process - *E-LOAN*
· Commercial	● Auto Loans: The Dealership Process - *GiggoCar*
· Credit Counseling	● Mortgages: What Kind of Loan Should You Get? - *SmartMoney*
· Financial Aid	● Auto Loans: Negotiation Tips - *GiggoCar*
· Financial Calculators	● Auto Loans: The Auto Loan Process - *GiggoCar*
	● Mortgages: Loan Purchase Strategies in Today's Market - *E-LOAN*

on the web

To complement the bounty of Yahoo! Finance, the Web offers an abundance of tools and information to help organize your financial life. The balance of this book details sound financial objectives and then teaches you how to use the best sites on the Web to reach your financial goals.

Automobiles: real wheels on the information super highway

Faced with the variety so carefully cultivated by the automobile industry, everyone in the market for a car wants exactly the same thing: The right car at the best price, nothing more. Yet too often they get a lot less. The odds of getting a fair deal on a car increase dramatically with the kind of research made easy by the Internet.

In recent years, car dealers have made a pronounced effort to turn brick and mortar automobile shopping into a more pleasant and equitable experience for customers. Apparently they didn't act quickly enough, because at the present time, 10 percent of new cars are sold through the Internet, and the number is growing. The irony is that customers are said to be paying more on average for new cars over the Internet than they would have paid the high-pressure salesman down at the local showroom. And so, as in any purchase, use the Internet to prepare yourself for the transaction, knowing just what you want, what a fair market price would be, and your opportunities for purchase.

step one: kicking the virtual tires
Choosing a model on the Internet's version of Automobile Row

A great many people who buy cars don't know their engine from their elbow. That makes life very easy for anybody who sells cars. The first thing for you to do as a buyer is simply to know about the advantages of the cars you want. You're bound to learn later, anyway, when you are behind the wheel—or far in front of it, in the passenger seat of a tow truck. The sites in this section give you a free preview of life with the car you think you want. Some of them are statistical, some editorial, but each in its own way describes the good

Insiders' Tour of Yahoo!—Autos
(autos.yahoo.com)

Yahoo! Autos can help you buy, sell, fix, maintain, or simply learn more about any make of car. To make the right purchasing decision, look at Buy a Car, and browse all the possibilities by make, class, or price. You can find complete model descriptions for any new or late-model used car, along with pricing. You can even compare multiple models using the "compare" feature.

TIP: More specific points of interest, such as performance statistics and color choices, can be found through a list at the end of the model descriptions. If you are uncertain about the buying process, How to Buy a Car is a step-by-step tutorial covering everything from negotiating to closing the deal.

If you are selling a car, Yahoo! Autos can help price it realistically, with variables for mileage, features, and special options. For selling or buying, Yahoo! Classified Ads list more than 1 million cars. Another popular way to deal a car online is through Yahoo! Auctions. **TIP: Both the classifieds and auctions at Yahoo! are free to use.**

Another useful feature of Yahoo! Autos is Personalized Services. Once you sign up, you can store your car's maintenance records online, access vehicle-specific recall information, and receive timely oil change reminders by e-mail.

TIP: These oil change reminders are a great complement to the Yahoo! Calendar, another handy Yahoo! tool.

points, the bad points and the just plain points of every new or late-model used car sold in America.

According to Autotrader.com, there are no less than 1,647 new car models on the market. In the category of used cars, there are 8,512 different types to choose from. To help narrow the field just a tad, Autotrader has designed a tool called the Decision Guide, which matches your answers to a series of about eight questions to a list of cars well-suited to you. For those of us who already know what we want, however, the questionnaire serves to confirm, rather than suggest, the right choice in cars. It took two or three tries, but I finally got the Decision Guide to advise me to buy a Porsche convertible.

Once you have narrowed down your wish list, Autotrader's site has a side-by-side comparison chart that enables you to survey up to four models at once. I compared three cars: a '96 Porsche convertible, a BMW M3 of the same year, and a rather less racy Ford truck. In a single glance, the comparison charts display current pricing, options and features, and ratings for safety and mileage. Having a model in mind, you can turn to Autotrader.com's greatest asset: 1.5 million actual cars, in the form of advertisements for used vehicles. The ads, drawn from *Auto Trader* magazines nationwide, can be sorted by region or even by neighborhood.

Autotrader.com

Corporate HQ Atlanta, Georgia

NO CHARGE   SEARCH   CALC.   QUOTES

new or used

The New Auto Comparison Chart on the Intellichoice website complements the used-car chart on Autotrader.com. Remarkably extensive, with detailed listings on pricing, taxes, dealer charges, specifications, options, safety, and performance, these customized comparison charts offer auto consumers a chance to do what they are supposed to do in any economy: create the setting for competition. With that in mind, I looked at my Porsche versus a Mercedes-Benz SLK two-seater: two cars quite similar in many ways as the eye glances down a list of numbers, but what a disparity in topspeed! And how easy it is to spot differences on such a chart. An offshoot of the annual *Complete Car Cost Guide* book series, Intellichoice.com does not sell cars, it exists to educate consumers—and to sell *Car Cost Guides*. Intellichoice's new-model list is probably the most extensive on the Internet, overlooking neither the Panoz AIV, nor the noticeably more common Ford F-150.

Intellichoice.com
Complete Car Cost Guide
Corporate HQ: Campbell, California

NO CHARGE   SEARCH   E-COM   CALC.

QUOTES

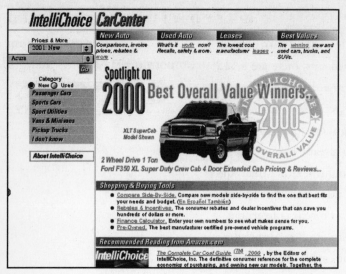

While its data on late-model used cars is also extensive (to see it all in one glance for any one model, click Expand to Print), the Intellichoice site also provides easily digestable information on aspects of the car-purchase decision slightly less glamorous than, say, topspeeds. A page devoted to national lease programs analyzes them down to the small print deals offered by manufacturers and ranks those carrying the lowest cost. Intellichoice updates the list at the beginning of each month. Another timely feature, which you'll find listed on the homepage, gives you a look at the salesman's version of hard candy, current consumer rebates and dealer incentives, as dictated by the manufacturers.

written reviews

Edmunds.com

Corporate HQ: Los Angeles, California

A car may be a machine, but there is more to it than numbers, specs and measurements. If you want to know about the indefinables, too, Edmunds, the car-magazine publisher, keeps its online file fresh with up-to-the-moment reviews. The writing is chatty and informative. Along with the reviews, Edmunds includes new car prices: both the dealer invoice and the suggested retail price, for each model and every option. The site's own model appraisals are linked directly to consumer comments, sorted neatly and quite specifically on Edmund's lively Town Hall message boards.

prices

KBB.com

Kelley Blue Book

Corporate HQ: Orange County, California

The Kelley Blue Book was started in 1926 by a Los Angeles used-car dealer, Les Kelley, who sent around a mimeographed flyer telling car dealers what he would pay them for used cars that they had taken in trade. Before long, car dealers around the country were depending on Mr. Kelley's book—colored blue when it was printed in book form—almost as though it were a legal document. Though tinged with a bit of the blarney of an old-time car salesman, the company's website offers hard facts by the millions. The most valuable tool for anyone who owns a car or wants one is the Used Car Valuator, which quotes two prices for any car you might profile. First, it lists the trade-in value (what you can expect a dealer to give you for it toward a new car) and second, it lists the retail price (what a dealer might charge for the same car).

The KBB data, which is based on actual transactions throughout the country, is also available for motorcycles, personal watercraft, and snowmobiles. KBB.com ranks the 50 most popular models among used and new cars, a list that is updated monthly.

If you aren't looking for information but an actual car, perchance, even one "way below book," then the real world is online at Cars.com. The biggest media syndicates in the country launched Cars.com and stuffed it with newspapers . . . specifically, the automobile classified ads from 130 dailies around the country. Searching for a car is easy, and much quicker than staring at long columns of small text over a bowl of cereal. Though it is not a quantifiable judgement, Cars.com seems to me to list the most interesting used cars on the Internet.

real-world values

Cars.com
Classified Ventures, Inc.
Corporate HQ: Chicago, Illinois

NO CHARGE

SEARCH

QUOTES

Though Cars.com counts its greatest strength in used-car ads, it has an array of tools and timely data directed toward the new-car purchase (a process that can be completed through the site's link to CarsDirect.com). You can use a calculator on the site to help clarify the difference between leasing a car and buying it outright. If you are indeed thinking about leasing a car, look at Cars.com's Automotive Lease Guide, which clarifies (and translates into understandable English), the legal fine print of contracts generated by each of the major manufacturers, clause by clause. You should also peruse the Manufacturer's Warranty Chart; it presents the terms offered by dozens of manufacturers—even Panoz! Cars.com is one of

Short shots

AutoWeek.com—manufacturer and model news
LemonAid.org—homegrown site with advice on poorly made cars
SmartCarGuide.com—basic car-buying tutorial

many automotive sites that links easily to Carfax.com, a service that checks a specific used car's service history, free of charge.

step two: driving a bargain
Buying a car on the Internet

Each of the sites in this step has developed its own distinct system for buying new cars over the Internet. They are worth examining, even if the thought of making a purchase of $10,000 or more online may be daunting at first. But then, because the specter of haggling over a car at a local dealership is also too daunting for a great many people, these services have become very popular of late.

locators

Autobytel.com

Corporate HQ: Irvine, California

NO CHARGE   SEARCH   E-COM   QUOTES

Autobytel sells cars—$1.4 million's worth per hour, according to the website. This is not some magical car lot, but a locator service, which means that just because Autobytel doesn't own any cars doesn't mean that it can't sell them. You have two choices on the site. The first is to pursue a purchase through a dealer: After plugging in the model you want, the site will generate a list of cars in your area fitting the basic description. You can look at the options and then choose to contact the dealership at which the car is located. Since Autobytel is affiliated with over 3,000 dealerships, the choice is usually wide. The second course is to pay Autobytel a fee of $129 in order to locate the car as described and then they will sell it to you. This course necessitates something considered unholy on most Internet sites—talking out loud. An Autobytel representative will use that old-fashioned device, the telephone, to consult with you about options, delivery and, most of all, about price. If a deal cannot be struck because Autobytel cannot supply exactly the car you want, then you get the whole $129 back. If you renege without getting your car for any other reason, you get $100 back.

letting the deal come to you

Like Autobytel, Stoneage represents a network of thousands of automobile dealerships. The difference between the sites lies in the impetus of the deal-making process. At Stoneage, you describe the car that you want, information that the site passes along as a lead to dealerships holding suitable cars. Once you hear from those dealerships, via the Internet or on the telephone, you are on your own in the deal-making process.

Stoneage.com

Corporate HQ: Troy, Michigan

completing the purchase online

DriveOff will quote an actual price on a new car and handle the sale for you. On the site, you describe the car you want and receive a quote immediately. As of this writing, the system was still being developed, and only the more popular models were available, not luxury or specialty cars. If you accept the price quote, DriveOff begins the process by exacting a $250 fee. Financing is also available as a step in that process, and requires an extra application. Within a few days, the company locates vehicles as described, usually offering a choice of color or features. You select one and receive an appointment to go and pick it up from a local dealership. DriveOff prides itself on having developed a means by which you can buy a car without ever speaking to a human being, a service it directs at customers who consider car salesmen only nominal members of the human species.

DriveOff.com

Navidec, Inc.

just one more thing . . .

CarSafety.org

HQ: Wells, Vermont

NO CHARGE   SEARCH

— Link List —

EAuto.com

A car once saved me. It had beams worthy of a railroad bridge on each side and when a sedan crashed full force against the door, the only affront to me was in the noise, which was very loud. The body repairman—for the car, not me—said that in practically any other car, I would have had to go to the hospital. Crash-worthiness may not be the only consideration in car buying, but it should certainly be near the top of your list. CarSafety.org culls data on crash tests from government and insurance-industry sources, knitting it into charts that grade models on a dozen aspects of accident protection. If you like, you can compare two different models, side-by-side. The site also offers background regarding each category of protection: In the section on overall death rates, for example, one important graph illustrates the records on that most desirable vehicle option—a driver that survives a crash. Other than high-performance cars, small-size SUV's had far and away the most deaths per million vehicles.

HwySafety.org also offers crash-safety evaluations, as does Insurance.com, which covers a more limited number of models.

Automobiles

* Start with the widest selection of vehicles possible; don't allow predispositions like color to start your list. The process of narrowing the choices will ultimately serve to inform your decision, letting you see more of the market and how your selection fits into it.

* Know all of the options available for a model, especially a used one, to ensure that you don't pay for something that you don't remotely want.

* Compare similar models side-by-side. It is the best way to see them both clearly.

* People who buy more of a car than they can afford to cover with collision and/or comprehensive insurance may end up making years' worth of payments on cars that will be repossesed. In setting your price limits, find out what complete insurance coverage will cost.

* Don't trust any single source for a price quote. If you are shopping online, phone a dealership. If you are working with a dealer, get a price from an online automobile broker. In either sphere, ask for prices from at least two sources.

Banking:
money in the abstract

Banking is only as local as you care to make it. Community banks are thriving today, but then, so are those looming products of megamerger, "banking institutions," recognizable not so much by their giant assets, but by their immediate adoption of meaningless names. Glistening new Internet banks have all sorts of names, from the lovely to the stark, but what they don't have are lobbies. You are your own teller in this new world. In the olden days of 1850 or 1950, one could judge the solidity of a bank just by the lobby. If it had chandeliers, its reputation was impeccable. However, without lobbies, there is no way to judge a bank for yourself. Making things worse is the constant temptation to deposit money far, far away, beyond even the regulatory effects of neighborhood word-of-mouth. And, all kidding aside, the need is more desperate than ever for help in evaluating the financial background of any bank in the country, help which the Internet can provide.

first step: rating any bank
Finding quality banking, and understanding it

Interest rates measure the value of money, whether it is money you deposit or borrow. They also measure your relationship with your bank and prescribe the activity you will be drawn to pursue. The first site in this step, Bankrate.com, studies interest rates nationwide across a variety of accounts and loans. Rates are one thing—ratings are another, though, when it comes to selecting a place to put your money. Some banks are distinctly better than others, more forthcoming in dealings with customers and more responsible in the safe management of assets. The subsequent sites in this step reveal the ways by which you can judge a bank, any bank, or benefit from the assessments of qualified examiners.

Insiders' Tour of Yahoo!—Banking
(banking.yahoo.com)

Through arrangements with selected banks in the United States and other countries, you can keep track of your bank accounts at Yahoo! Finance. If you are shopping for a bank with online services, a section called Banking Scorecards offers a list of the 20 top banks, as judged by Gomez Advisors. The banks are also rated by specific categories, such as ease of use and overall cost.

The Rates page lists the interest rates currently being paid or charged throughout the country. The basic categories are savings deposits, personal loans, auto loans, and mortgages, each of which lists rates on a variety of accounts or loans. **TIP: Under More Rates in the Auto Loan and Mortgage sections, you can find regional interest rates, specific to states and major cities.**

Yahoo! Finance's Banking Center also provides calculators to assist you

in evaluating your use of credit cards, savings and Individual Retirement accounts (IRAs). Yahoo! Bill Pay (billpay.yahoo.com) is a fast growing service that allows you to pay you bills without paper checks.

NO CHARGE   E-COM   CALC.

numbers up-to-date

Bankrate.com
Corporate HQ: North Palm Beach, Florida

NO CHARGE   SEARCH   CALC.

The only thing that all modern banks have in common is that they offer rates on the use of your money. The matter of rates represents a single black line amid the wide, white space of banking today. On it, all the banks sit like crows, bickering and barking, but sitting still, right out in the open. And Bankrate.com watches them, like Aesop's fox.

The site monitors 102 types of loans and savings vehicles, and can give you the national average, the top five rates nationwide, or the best rates for your locale. These statistics are surrounded at every turn by enthusiastic editorial content, which tends to lean more toward the direction of Internet banks, than "brick-and-mortar" ones. One perfectly objective feature is a chart describing the services and fees of more than thirty Internet banks; for quick comparison go to Online Finance from the homepage and find the "Online Banks and Fees" button. Bankrate.com regularly reviews online banking sites, but only as *sites*; evaluations of the underlying services are more sporadic. Arguably the most comprehensive of all the banking sites aimed at consumers, Bankrate.com can be used as a starting point for online finance, or as a slide rule by which to measure your current service.

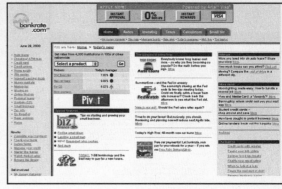

Bauer Financial is a rating service that is, itself, highly rated. Generating an array of financial research, mostly for institutional customers, though at no charge, the company's site offers visitors an initial assessment of any institution. According to the site, any bank receiving either four or five stars (out of five) receives Bauer's recommendation. If you prefer, you can type in the name of a city and see the star ratings on every bank headquartered there. Denver, for example, drew a list of 18 institutions (seven of which, large and small, received the highest rating). You can order a complete statistical report online for $20, though some banks arrange with BauerFinancial to release their reports at no charge (two, for example, on the Denver listing did so).

BauerFinancial.com

Corporate HQ: Coral Gables, Florida

NO CHARGE   SEARCH   E-COM

in-depth reports

Veribanc is one of the older bank-rating services, dating back to 1981, which was, not coincidentally, the eve of the nation's savings and loan disaster—a collapse that Veribanc claims it foresaw. The service limits itself to ratings of retail banks, including S&L's, holding companies, and credit unions. There is both a color code for the institution's current stability and a star ranking for its future outlook. As the site explains, you can learn the ratings of any institution by phone, mail, or fax for $10.

    We recommend that you seriously consider ordering a written research report on your bank, especially if it is distant and not otherwise known to you. You can order

Veribanc.com

Corporate HQ: Wakefield, Massachusetts

E-COM

such reports from either BauerFinancial.com ($20) or Veribanc.com at a cost of $28—and if you can't afford that, you can't afford to be fooling around with faraway banks. Veribanc tailors its reports to individuals, explaining its data in plain English.

Some banks which receive the highest grades in both of Veribanc's categories, and which exhibit other qualities as well, are designated "Blue Ribbon Banks." Veribanc watches over its flock of Blue Ribbon winners and boasts that not one has ever failed. For $38, you can order the most recent list of Blue Ribbon Banks for any region.

bank scams

FDIC.gov
Federal Deposit Insurance
Corporation
HQ: Washington, D.C.

NO CHARGE   SEARCH   ARCHIVE

Most people put their money in banks, while some put it in "Entities That May Be Conducting Banking Operations." That's not a bank. The FDIC has enough trouble keeping bad banks from wrecking people's lives. When it comes to "Entities," the agency can do little but warn the public that there is nothing more slippery in the world, including frogs.

Without wishing to encourage anyone to enter the field, I suggest that the Internet has probably made life very, very easy for Entities That May Be Conducting Banking Operations. But on second thought, that is not fair at all: What makes life easy for Entities is an ill-informed person who is a trifle too excited by high rates of return. Since that phrase describes practically everyone I know, the best advice around is to make double sure that your bank is recognized by the FDIC—you can do that at FDIC.gov. Continue your research by looking at whatever further data the FDIC offers on the bank, and by understanding the limitations of FDIC insurance, also explained on the site.

step two: deciding on an online bank
Whether you want one and where it should be

As the sites in this step explain, banking on the Internet can be conducted at a number of different levels. They range from traditional banks, which simply offer customers the chance to view their accounts online, to fully committed online banks, institutions that transact business only through the Internet. Each ascending level tends to require more preparation for both the customer and for his or her computer. BankInfo.com describes the latest trends, while Money.com rates the top institutions, and SFNB.com offers a worthwhile demonstration for those still considering their aptitude for online banking. An Internet specialty related to banking, and sometimes offered with it, is automatic bill paying. It has yet to catch on in a big way, but you can measure its convenience for yourself in the demonstrations listed at the end of Step Two.

Short shots

BanxQuote.com—updated rates for any bank
CreativeInvest.com—Minority-owned banks
ePayNews.com/glossary—e-banking jargon
FreeATMs.com—locator for no-fee automatic teller machines

industry viewpoint

BankInfo.com
Thomson Financial Publishing
Corporate HQ: Skokie, Illinois

 NO CHARGE   ARCHIVE

BankInfo.com is actually a bank . . . of articles. They are largely directed at bankers, which is why it is an especially beneficial place for consumers to go and eavesdrop. The most telling section of the site is the Online Banking Series, with pieces on the various ways in which people are using home computers to maintain their bank accounts. Unlike most sites, BankInfo.com is not necessarily gung-ho on the Internet, at least not on Internet banks. Without being against them, either, it is just very, very conservative in making its judgements. That conservatism is a sterling attribute in a world which should have no fads, no breezes, and certainly no gusts that come to nothing: in other words, banking, the world that protects your savings.

test runs

Money.com
Corporate HQ: New York City, New York

 NO CHARGE   ARCHIVE   CALC.

To conduct its ongoing Survey of Internet Banks (found on the homepage), Money.com does what few sites have the wherewithal to do: open and operate actual accounts. In the most recent survey, Money.com, which is an adjunct to *Money* magazine, tried 23 Internet banks. It evaluated them on rates and fees; deposits and checking; customer service; bill paying, and security. The survey goes beyond the site reviews on BankRate.com, because it describes the experience of dealing with each institution in fuller dimension: the dimension of use. With its excellent survey, Money.com is a launch-pad for any search for an Internet bank. It does not, however, pre-tend to vouch for the financial solidity of the banks that are rated. All of them are major institutions—not Entities—but it is your task to investigate the integrity of the banks you like. (See Step One.)

demonstration

SFNB.com

Security First Network Bank

Corporate HQ: Atlanta, Georgia

NO CHARGE   E-COM

SFNB boasts of being the first true Internet bank, having been founded in October of 1995. That fact may or may not put it in a league with the Bank of New York, which was founded in 1784 (and is America's oldest private bank). But what is even more unique about SFNB is that it was the first Internet bank to open a "brick-and-mortar" office, to boot. The main office is in Cyberspace, the branch is in the Buckhead section of greater Atlanta. Those of us who appreciate the Internet, but root for the real world every time, are putting that branch in *our* history books. While this book does not recommend any specific institutions as repositories for your money, it is advisable for anyone flirting with the idea of opening an account at an online bank to run the thorough demonstration that is offered at SFNB.com. The demo does not over-simplify, but uses a sensible degree of anima-tion to take you through the processes of maintaining a check-ing account, using credit cards, paying bills online, and so forth.

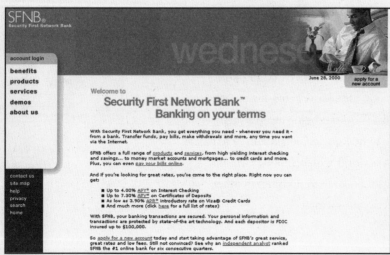

automatic bill-paying

Checkfree.com

Corporate HQ: Atlanta, Georgia

NO CHARGE   E-COM

Most online banks and a few independent sites offer bill-paying services, which allow you to direct remittances via your computer. Some services go further than that, in actually collecting your mail and notifying you of payments due. And some go even a bit further than that, in accepting bills electronically from your creditors. The silliest benefit touted for e-payment is that with it, you won't have to put stamps on envelopes any longer (anybody that lazy should be tested for signs of life). The most attractive benefit, though, is that you can handle your bills even when traveling, through the use of the Internet. Somewhere in between these two advantages is the fact that stray bills won't clutter up your kitchen counters, ever again. For those wanting a test drive, Checkfree.com offers a demonstration of e-paying. BankRate.com reports regularly on the field and its players, all developing rapidly and hoping to find a mammoth market.

Link List

BankInfo.com—quicklinks
Bank2000.com—worldwide bank links
CuLand.com—credit unions
OnlineBankingReport.com—resources

---

just one more thing . . .

CUNA.org
Credit Union National Association

HQ: Washington, D.C.

NO CHARGE   SEARCH   ARCHIVE

Credit Unions have long been the "me too" institutions of retail banking. They don't receive much publicity, because they are restricted by law to serve a specific group of people—most often, employees of a certain company or members of a certain club. Fees, which are already low in most cases, are sometimes further reduced through volunteer staffing by members. CUNA.org has a Consumer Info section with answers to common questions, such as finding a credit union to join. With the Internet, credit unions can extend membership to wider groups, geographically, at least.

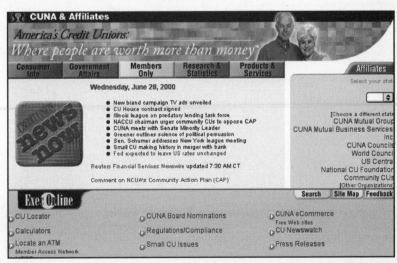

Banking

* Make an effort to see beyond your own accounts, and conduct an ongoing evaluation of the bank's management. Inefficiently operated banks are not only dangerous as caretakers of your money, they may be more likely than other banks to withhold it wherever possible.

* Too many people, especially those who bank online, overlook the help that a good banker can offer as part of the service included with any account. Whatever kind of bank you prefer, develop a relationship with a banker, one who will be familiar with your accounts and can periodically advise you on ways to streamline or improve them.

* Know the fees charged by your bank. Charges for common services are too often obscure, if not hidden, which is one reason they seem to grow larger with each passing year.

* Try Internet banking in stages, making sure that you understand it completely before committing all of your funds to an online account.

Consumerism and charity: good living

A lot of sites on the Internet seem altruistic. Whether or not you can trust any of them is another matter. Earning money, saving money; doubling it in stocks or watching it grow in an account . . . your thrifty ways are not going to matter if you are simultaneously getting bilked. The steps in this chapter focus on three of the most common ways to get fooled. The first one pertains to purchases, the second to brokerages, and the third to charities.

One of the exhilarating aspects of the Internet, and indeed of the modern economy as a whole, is the wide range of choices offered in the three categories above. Innovation is keen, "change" is a hallowed word, and all manner of transactions are accelerated, if not rushed. However, with decisions made on the fly, and with the general encouragement to try new ways and to trust new companies, consumers are especially vulnerable to disappointments, the kind that can be measured in dollars. Bad people say good-sounding things on the web; this chapter helps you to see them for who they are.

step one: advance scouting
With the Internet at hand, there is no excuse for consumer ignorance

A bad product can be returned, and a service that is unacceptable can be cancelled for a refund, but only if these things were sold by an honorable company. On the Internet or off of it, there is no reason to trust a company with a poor reputation, or one that refuses

So You Want to Be an Online Trader

The Internet has turned us into a nation of brokers. I don't recall any of my schoolmates in grade school expressing a dream of becoming a stockbroker someday: an airline pilot and a jockey, maybe. Yet, becoming an instant self-broker is the latent dream that has been realized for millions of people through the proliferation of online brokerages. To many, that is what "Internet finance" is all about: the freedom to invest or to trade in only a few key strokes. But freedom in this case is just another word for a lot more to lose. That seems like a gloomy outlook, but the fact is that in any market, good or bad, market advice that is underscored by expertise, research, and experience is worth quite a lot.

One thing is certain. You will no doubt handle your account better than a bad broker would. To handle it better than an average or excellent broker, however, you will have to do more than merely pick stocks. You will have to equip yourself to understand the choices and possibilities within any investment vehicle and for any market condition. You ought to think through anything that might happen with any of your investments—for example, any convertible issue—and stand prepared with contingency plans. Familiarize yourself with tax implications of your investments and try to think through the issues of timing that bear upon them. A good broker is a lookout and a source of advice on all such concerns; no one should trade independently online who is not prepared to take on the same matters.

And no one should trade online simply because it is less bother to do so than to find a first-rate broker.

to follow the standards of fair business practice. The first site in this step, Consumer.gov, describes the parameters for fair practice in many different businesses and informs you of the furtive or even dangerous ways that some companies are skirting them. The next two sites, those of J.D. Power and the Better Business Bureau, cite specific companies for standards that are high or low—or nonexistent.

It is our government's job to protect fools, bumpkins, and dopes, which is why there is something for everyone on the federal site devoted to consumer advice. A welcoming hub, Consumer.gov scans hundreds of other government websites, categorizing and linking all of the pages containing tips or timely warnings. The top of the homepage offers a choice of 10 categories: food, transportation, money, product safety, and so forth. Each leads to a choice of sub-categories, though the editors also choose some linked pages to feature either In the Spotlight, or among the Scam Alerts collected for certain categories.

Before making any momentous purchase over the Internet, hunt around Consumer.gov for an advisory. For example, don't order important medication on the Internet until you have read "Internet Purchase of Prescription Drugs: Buyer Beware," a page originating on the Food and Drug Administration site. (At Consumer.gov, the piece can be located by clicking Health, and then Medical Products Online.) The article, full of sobering medical facts, reported on a study of 37 drugstore sites. According to the report, the average cost of common medications was actually higher online than it was at real drugstores surveyed in Philadelphia. (Any person who is now wondering whether it still wouldn't be cheaper to buy prescriptions online than to go to Philadelphia for them *is* beyond help.)

hard lessons
Consumer.gov
U.S. government
HQ: Washington D.C.

NO CHARGE

ARCHIVE

buyer experience
JDPower.com
J.D. Power and Associates
Corporate HQ: Los Angeles, California

NO CHARGE

SEARCH

In 1968, J.D. Power III had the radical idea of finding out about consumer satisfaction by asking the consumers what they thought. Manufacturers, especially in the automobile field, grew to depend on the information for product planning. In the mid-1980s, they started to use it in advertising, too, and J.D. Power and Associates became a household name. The company does not make recommendations, it only totes the results and issues rankings. Because the J.D. Power company knows how to ask questions and how to analyze answers, its surveys are much more revealing than the scattershot consumer feedback that often falls into other websites. The Hot off the Press searching tool provides access to reports in the

form of press releases. Type in online, for a choice that includes a survey conducted on Internet brokerages.

reputations

BBB.org
Council of Better Business Bureaus
HQ: Arlington, Virginia

NO CHARGE

SEARCH

Most of the local Better Business Bureaus in the country cooperate with a nationwide database: If you need background information on any particular company, you can type in a name or phone number and see whether or not the firm has been investigated by a BBB. If it has, the report can include anything from the barest name and address, to a list of company managers and perhaps observations of the company's dealings. Not all reports are bad, by any means, but the ones that are critical can make you shudder. If you are looking

for a type of business, a roofing company, for example, you can search a specific industry according to locale. The BBB sponsors a separate site, BBBOnline.org, dedicated to promoting reliability and respect for privacy on the Internet. There are also succinct tips for online shopping, even, or especially, at those sites without the BBB seal of approval.

step two: bearing down on investing

Before you trust a nickel to an online firm, know exactly who's at the other end of the Net

The sites in this step introduce investors to the obligations and opportunities attached to trading online. There is more on this topic in Chapter XII, which takes a hard look at online brokerages. In this step, we are hoping you will take a hard look at yourself, to ascertain the strengths you bring to Internet finance, and the ones you can develop through the Internet.

judging yourself as an online investor

InvestingOnline.org
Investing Online Resource Center
HQ: Olympia, Washington

NO CHARGE

The State of Washington Department of Financial Institutions considers online investing to be in some senses a fad, and potentially a dangerous one. "How could it possibly be a fad?" you may be scoffing. "Everybody's doing it."

Even people at the State of Washington Department of Financial Institutions are doing it, no doubt, but that still doesn't make it right for every type of investor. The Investing Online Resource Center, a project of that department, set up its website to try and help people gauge their own ability to manage all aspects of a portfolio. The site, OnlineInvesting.org, starts with a quiz to test your suitability in that regard. Should you pass, it next offers a list of Eight Things You Should Know: No. 5 being, for example, "Limit-orders are a must," and No. 4, "Costs may not always be obvious."

the view from washington

SEC.gov
Securities & Exchange Commission
HQ: Washington D.C.

NO CHARGE   SEARCH   CALC.   ARCHIVE

Everyone who passes OnlineInvesting's little quiz should go directly to a speech made by Arthur Leavitt, chairman of the SEC, in May 1999. In it, he covered the subject of online trading as it pertains to the individual investor, from the absurdity of brokerage advertising, to the wonderful freedom of the overall system. Leavitt acknowledges all of the strengths and pitfalls—and so should you—before you hire yourself as your own broker. The speech is featured on the SEC website (under sec.gov.news/speeches/spch274.html). Under the general topic of Investor Assistance and Education, the site offers online trading tips, including detailed advice on day trading and the three questions you need to ask yourself to avoid online investing scams. If you are thinking about filing a complaint regarding an investment broker, SEC.gov wants the facts in a form it can use later: Hence, there are lessons on how to take notes during a conversation with a bad broker.

You might be taken aback to notice a reference to the Connecticut Council on Problem Gambling. The haunting reason for that unlikely link is that the Council has developed a test to determine just what it is you are doing with your online trading: investing or gambling.

broker ratings

Gomez.com
Gomez Advisors
Corporate HQ: Lincoln, Massachusetts

NO CHARGE

SEARCH

Gomez.com provides what it calls "decision support." (I think that means *advice,* among the capable jargon.) Gomez was one of the Internet's first overview sites, offering objective profiles of online brokerages. The information was originally presented in dull charts, which, nonetheless, thrilled early websurfers because the Gomez charts showed at a single glance both how much there was on the Internet in terms of brokerages and how quickly online data could be absorbed. Now that those two sensations are yesterday's news, Gomez.com has broken up the charts, giving each of the top firms in any one field its own bright dossier of figures and rankings, along with a couple of paragraphs in summary. In addition to brokerages, Gomez.com offers decision support regarding an array of sites: banks, airlines, apparel, and others.

Some of the rankings are far from enlightening. Gomez's top choice among online booksellers is, catch your breath, Amazon.com. The top auction service is Ebay. I can't expect Gomez to push some smaller site forward, just for the sake of sprightly reading, but such choices show how entrenched online leaders have become. When Gomez.com started, no one knew the players, let alone the stars: Common knowledge of the "best" websites in each field will only render Gomez, itself, obsolete. As you peruse the information available on Gomez.com, be aware that the company earns revenue through affiliations with many of the online companies under scrutiny. For example, seven of the online broker-

ages ranked in the site's top 10 participate in its affiliation program, giving special deals to registered Gomez users. Whether or not such relationships sully the objectivity of the rankings is for you to decide.

timing brokerage service

Keynote.com

Keynote Systems

Corporate HQ: San Mateo, California

NO CHARGE

On Keynote.com's site, charts rank online brokerages as though they were race cars. The first specification given for each is the 0-to-60 time; that is, the transaction time. The second is the topspeed, or the transaction success rate. Keynote Systems, the company behind the site, uses computer testing to measure the quality of service of Internet websites. For consumers, the Brokerage Trading Index shows, in the bluntest of terms, the service you can expect from each online firm. If you intend to trade stocks with the pedal to the metal, then it will be of great interest to you to see transaction times carried out to the hundredth of a second—just think of all the money to be made an hour! The transaction success rate, as of this writing, varied from about 50 percent to 90 percent on Keynote's rankings.

step three: the privilege of charity

Be as smart in giving your money away as you are in earning it

Be especially careful in giving money to charity; the crooks in that field know how to sound good in more ways than one. We would be sorry to see you waste your money on a scam, while some effective charity went wanting at the very same time. The first site in this step, Newtithing.org, gives you some perspective on personal donations in this country. The sites in the next entry help you to find and research large charities and tiny ones. Both WebCharity and the Humane Society encourage charitable spending: using your purchasing power to good effect.

Short shots

Dma.org/consumers/off-mailinglist.html—The Direct Marketing Association will remove your name from contact lists

Eff.org—The Electronic Frontier offers 12 Ways to Protect Your Privacy Online

assessing your giving

Newtithing.org
Newtithing Group
HQ: San Francisco, California

NO CHARGE

CALC.

Once you have honed your skills as a stock trader and surpassed poor old John Rockefeller, you will probably want to do as he did and give your money away. And even if you don't want to, you know you should. Newtithing Group has set itself up as a sort of cattle prod in an era of prosperity: giving a little push to tailbones, especially among the herd of newly rich. A calculator on Newtithing.org's homepage will helpfully inform you of the amount you can afford to donate. According to another page, which profiles giving by income bracket, those who earn $25,000 to $49,999 have an estimated $3,400 in discretionary funds; they can afford $675 in annual donations and, according to IRS records, make actual donations of only $480. For purposes of comparison, the group also ranks the states, according to this affordable/actual formula on donations. Utah is the best of the lot, as its richer citizens hand off about 68 percent of what they can afford to give. Delaware has much deeper pockets, according to the ranking, in which it finished last.

Link List

ConsumerWorld.com
CyberInvest.com
Epic.org—Resources, links on Internet privacy issues
http://nccs.urban.org/links.htm#Biblio—charity links

charities in need

GuideStar.com
Philanthropic Research Inc.
Corporate HQ: Williamsburg, Virginia

NO CHARGE

SEARCH

Assuming that you want to donate fully 110 percent of what you can afford to give, GuideStar.com always knows someone who could use your help. The site keeps a database of 620,000 charities that can be searched by objective, locale, or name. However, GuideStar.com does not evaluate these charities on their merit or integrity. Once you have a list of some decent-sounding, non-profit groups, you can conduct further research by going to the website of the National Center for Charitable Statistics in Washington. The complete address is http://NCCS.urban.org. At that site, you can order a download of the IRS form filed by any charity. In addition, the Better Business Bureau, listed above at BBB.org, keeps records on complaints filed about charitable organizations. Finally, you ought to contact the attorney general of your state; most of them keep a watchful eye on nonprofits. The National Fraud Information Center, at NFIC.org, has links to the sites maintained by each state's attorney general.

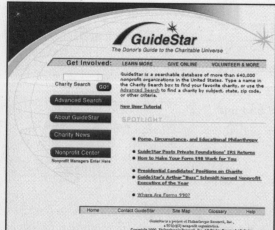

If you are more casual about giving your money, then by all means, give it to me. Otherwise, go through the steps of learning just exactly how your donation will be spent and by whom. And if that is too much work, then I'd say that the odds of some smart-aleck somewhere buying a new Porsche with your hard-earned money just got a whole lot better.

fund-raising auction site

WebCharity.com
Corporate HQ: Branford, Connecticut

WebCharity is one of several sites that have forged into the field of e-white elephant sales. In lists of nine main categories, items from automobiles (a vintage fire truck, for example) to food (gourmet olive oil), are donated by individuals or companies around the country. The proceeds benefit one of the 600 charities registered with the site, although the amount of the sale earmarked for the charity can vary from 100 percent down to a piddling 10 percent. In any case, WebCharity assumes for itself 10 percent off the very top, so you should keep in mind that while great good is done by the site, it is nonetheless a commercial one, and very much for-profit.

finding companies that care

HSUS.org
Humane Society of the United States
HQ: Washington D.C.

The Humane Society site covers timely animal rights issues on its website's homepage. It also watches over consumer issues of special interest to those people who try to influence the world, not merely through what they donate or do, but through what they purchase, as well. On the pull-down menu of animal issues, for example, is a page on Cosmetics Testing. Now that synthetic means are readily available to conduct cosmetics testing, it seems a travesty to kill cats and other animals in that pursuit. According to the Humane Society, however, some cosmetics companies are claiming on labels to use animal-free testing, when they really do sacrifice little beings. One of the many consumer alerts at HSUS.org is a list of those companies that have signed the Corporate Standard of Compassion for Animals, a covenant that closes all the loopholes.

just one more thing . . .

Anonymizer.com

Corporate HQ: LaMesa, California

NO CHARGE

Yahoo! quote

The revolution in technology is dramatically changing the entire competitive landscape. Before long, it won't be just the brokers and banks and insurance companies. In a sense, we're all software providers, and you can't help wondering if the phone company, the electric company, or the hardware store on the corner will one day be a competitor.

—Charles Schwab III, chairman and CEO, Charles Schwab & Co. Interview in *Think* magazine, www.IBM.com/thinkmag/archive/archive2/schwab1

Be warned: The name of this website is almost unpronounceable. Perhaps that is part of the idea, its founders preferring such things as names to remain unsaid. The site was launched from an idea contained in the United Nations Universal Declaration of Human Rights, which stated that "None shall be subjected to arbitrary interference with his privacy, family, home, or correspondence." To that end, Anonymizer sells software for avid Netsurfers: One package called Window Washer automatically erases the trail you leave every time you visit a website. As a free service, Anonymizer.com invites people to surf the Net or send e-mail under its aegis, so as to shield their privacy. The unfortunate fact is that prying eyes line the great information highway, and privacy has been largely sacrificed in the mad rush to—well, I'm still not positive what we're rushing to. But I do know that we'll have no secrets left by the time we get there.

Consumerism and Charity

The Long and Short of

* Tracing the reputation of a company is essential. If those associated with the company are proud of their record, they will be glad you made inquiries.

* Research any company that contacts you (through the mail, the Internet, or the telephone), before you agree to a purchase.

* Before you open an account at an online brokerage, consider your ability to handle the many different situations that may arise.

* Every investment that you make requires your own independent research and judgement—do not let anyone rush you into an investment.

* Many crooked operators will contact you by telephone or on the Internet to pressure you into some "stupendous" investment opportunity. See it in writing and corroborate all the facts for yourself. If you don't have the time or resources to thoroughly investigate obscure investments, then turn them down.

* *Don't take candy or investments from strangers.* If you do not have a broker, accountant, or lawyer, ask your banker to take a look at investments people are trying to sell you.

* Before donating money to an unfamiliar charity, confirm that your donation will actually make it to the needy.

Credit:
the muscle behind your money

Loans, mortgages, and that ongoing bit of borrowing known as the credit card account are all means of extending your fortune. Or obliterating it. This chapter describes the import of your credit record and the most common types of loans taken out today. In great corporations, the proper use of credit is very often the difference between success and failure. Even more important, it is often the difference between ease and unhappiness in individuals.

The goal of this chapter is to introduce you quite objectively to yourself: your spending habits, attitudes, and available assets. At the same time, you have to know how others currently perceive you on those very counts. When those two jibe in the credit world, or in any other aspect of your life, the result is tranquility. When ignorance is mustered as a substitute, the result is bitter frustration, possible calamity, and long waits on hold, while you try to patch up your credit over the telephone.

From a different point-of-view, credit is really like any other commodity, silk or wine or rugs: There is a decided range in quality. This chapter can help you to insist upon the best for yourself, first finding out how to judge credit as though it were anything else you might purchase.

step one: see what they're saying about you
Credit reports determine how popular you will be with lenders

Reporting agencies keep a record of your spending habits, and the care you take in repaying loans of all types. The first two sites in this step help you to see the reports that have been compiled about you, and to analyze or even respond to the data in them. If

Insiders' Tour of Yahoo!—Credit
(loan.yahoo.com)

The Yahoo! Finance Loan Center is chockful of information on most types of loans. The mortgage center, for example, uses your answers to 10 simple questions to point you toward the right type of mortgage and then enables you to receive a quote on the mortgage you need. Another type of loan available through Yahoo! Finance is the small business loan. The Auto Loan Center also has a number of calculators to get you off to the right start in financing a car. One helps you to decide between leasing and buying, for example, while another analyzes the right amount of time to keep a particular car. **TIP: The Auto Loan Center has two articles helpful for those new to car-buying: a step-by-step tutorial on How to Buy a Car, and an article covering the Basics of Auto Loans.**

In 30 seconds, Yahoo! Finance can provide you with an online copy of your credit report. The charge of $7.95 also allows you to then track changes in the report over the course of the next four weeks. For a higher charge of $29.95, you can order credit reports from the three major credit agencies through Yahoo! Finance.

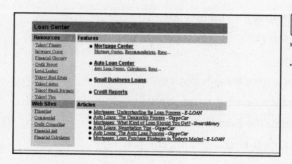

your spending habits have spun out of control, or if the care you took in repaying loans has lapsed, then your credit will have to be mended, and the next three sites in Step One offer help in varying degrees to that end.

Experian.com
Corporate HQ: Nottingham, England and Orange, California

At last count, Experian maintained a storehouse of 14 trillion bytes of information—at least a little something on 95 million households in America. Experian, which is a British company, also keeps data on people from other countries. Click on United States, on the homepage, and you can see a sample of one of its reports: denoting what "John Q. Consumer" bought and where, and whether payments were made in a timely manner. That little teaser may either make you want to see what Experian has on you or may make you vaguely uncomfortable, like catching sight of yourself in a mirror. In any case, you should peruse your credit report every two years: your credit *reports* (plural), that is. Experian is only one of three national data collection agencies, and, normally, a major creditor will seek reports from all three. The other two agencies are Trans-Union (TUC.com; Chicago, Illinois) and Equifax (Equifax.com; Atlanta, Georgia). All three agencies will allow you to order your report online, at prices that range up to about $8.50, depending on your circumstances and the state in which you live.

The challenge all the way through the process is security. As Experian put it—or was it Samuel Beckett—"If we cannot determine that the person requesting your credit report is really you, then we will not accept the purchase request." You may have been waiting your whole life for someone to determine that you are really you. Equifax's method is to ask a series of tricky questions.

You have a choice at all three agencies between viewing the report online or having it mailed: If you can bear the suspense, have it mailed. It will stand as an official document that way, should there be any problem with it, and the use of the mail will close one potential security leak.

CreditScoring.com
Corporate HQ: Dayton, Ohio

In recent years, credit reporting agencies have developed formulas by which they can sum up your credit-worthiness in one simple, three-digit number: the credit score. If the basic specter of monolithic reporting agencies serves to shrink the average American down to a pile of bytes, then credit-scoring dashes rugged individualism for good. The idea of credit scores offends many people. Considering

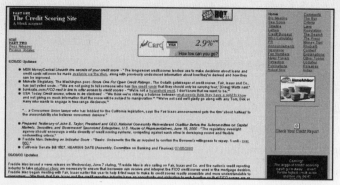

that the big credit-rating agencies have grown to be bigger than government in the sphere of personal finance, it is right to hear an opposing view and CreditScoring.com, a little David of a site, does its best to report on the credit-reporting Goliaths.

advice on credit

CCCSIntl.org
Consumer Credit Counseling
Service of the Gulf Coast Area
Corporate HQ: Houston, Texas

Though sponsored by a local Texas organization, CCCSIntl.com offers answers to a general array of credit questions. It is aimed at those people in danger of sliding inadvertently into credit problems—in other words, everybody. The site has an Account Balancer, an interactive tool with which you can balance your checkbook on a regular basis. The Know Your Rights section, written by a law dean, discusses specific cases as submitted by readers: For example, "Everything my wife and I have is in her name. She says I will get nothing if we divorce." (According to the dean: It will probably get split in half, no matter whose name it is in.)

counseling online

MMIntl.org
Money Management International
HQ: Houston, Texas

The credit experts in Houston have an affiliated agency that can tend to serious credit problems: In fact, Money Management International is operated by a consortium of six Consumer Credit Counseling Service regionals, including the one in Houston. Its site gets right down to business, offering a unique program of credit counseling, which is nonetheless rigorous for being conducted online. The service includes the development of a debt management plan, intervention with creditors, and the establishment of an account, managed by the agency, for bill payment.

For those who would prefer to meet in person with a credit counselor, NFCC.org maintains an online referral service of 1,450 Neighborhood Financial Centers all over the country. Even for people looking to mend their credit ways without outside help, the site features several debt calculators, some linked to other sites. The homegrown Budget and Debt test is probably the most helpful of all: It is a test to chart the direction in which you're headed, toward more savings or more debt, and how fast you're going.

NFCC.org
National Foundation for Credit Counseling
HQ: Silver Spring, Maryland

NO CHARGE   CALC.

step two: card games
Credit cards are carefully marketed to seem as though they represent money, when what they represent is a very serious type of loan

For all of the people who carry credit cards, or who are carried by them in the financial sense, very few fully understand the ramifications of credit-card use. The first site in this step, one produced by the Federal Reserve Board, offers a perky discussion of the various types of credit cards and their suitability for those in different situations. The second site, CardWeb.com, is blatantly commercial, but offers you a chance to compare cards of all types. The right credit card can plug a totally unnecessary drain on your money, including the drip-drip-drip found in fees, rates, and the means by each of them is calculated on your card. Recognizing the best kind of card for your particular habits is half the battle; finding the best one of that general kind makes up the other half of the battle—one well worth winning.

The Federal Reserve Board uses debt on the grand scale as a tiller by which to steer the national economy. It knows all about the nuances of taking on debt—and the chasms to which it can lead. Under the category of Consumers, the Board's site contains street-smart information on car leases and mortgages, and on the subject of shopping for a credit card. You can see at a glance how different variables will impact your ultimate cost on credit card debt. There

BOG.FRB.Fed.us
Board of Governors of the Federal Reserve System
HQ: Washington, D.C.

NO CHARGE   CALC.   ARCHIVE

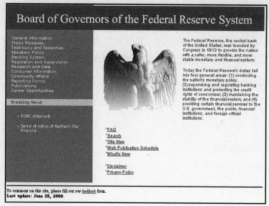

is also a four-step checklist on finding the best credit card. Even after you have found the very best credit card, the Board advises you to negotiate to make it even better.

current credit card offers

CardWeb.com

Corporate HQ: Frederick, Maryland

NO CHARGE

SEARCH

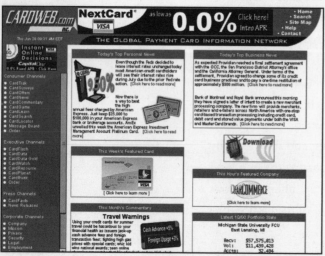

After your briefing from the Federal Reserve Board, you will know the jargon and know what kind of card would suit your spending practices best. The next step is to locate just such a card. Although the Federal Reserve Board site offers a survey of credit card rates and features, the print is quite small and you may find it easier to use the CardTrak surveys found at CardWeb.com. It ranks going offers in 12 categories, including cards with no fees, low rates, or reward programs. Another commercial site that monitors current credit-card offerings is bankrate.com (see Banking).

step three: a loan of your own
The Internet is a marketplace for lenders

— Short shots —

FreeCreditAnalyzer.com— gives a ballpark idea of your credit score, based on a short quiz

The Internet makes a surprisingly simple exercise of a formerly off-putting ceremony: requesting a loan. Applications are simple, and quotes are returned instantly, so that you can calculate, at the very least, whether or not your plans are realistic. If you want to proceed with an actual application for a loan, each of the sites in this step follows its own system. Whether or not you opt to apply online, the supporting information that each site offers will help you, nonetheless, to organize your application and understand the overall process of lending—and borrowing.

all about online lending

CreditLand.com
Corporate HQ: San Francisco, California

NO CHARGE CALC. QUOTES ARCHIVE

E-COM

Despite the dismaying snap of the funhouse in its name, Credit-Land.com is a solid site, with information on topics such as Your Credit Report and Fees and More (credit cards). Best of all, each topic contains a glossary. Among the many tools on the site is a calculator that helps you to ascertain how much you could save by transferring your balance to a card with a lower APR, or annual percentage rate. To pay its own debts, if it has any, CreditLand.com earns money as an Internet aggregator. While it does not extend credit, it will locate a lender for you online. The service is free for the customer; revenue is derived from the lenders who receive leads from CreditLand.

all types of loans

E-Loan.com
Corporate HQ: Dublin, California

NO CHARGE CALC. QUOTES E-COM

E-Loan represents 70 lending institutions around the country, and acts as an agent in setting up a loan for you with one of them. However, you do not have to be ready to sign on the dotted line in order to take advantage of E-Loan.com. Without so much as taking your name, the site will generate a list of actual lenders for you in all different types of loans. For example, to shop the rates for an automobile loan, you need only denote a state, loan amount, and model. A home loan requires the answers to nine questions. For either, you will see a chart of potential lenders and the rates they would charge. Should you choose to pursue a contract through E-Loan.com, a representative will work with you directly, online and over the telephone.

letting lenders bid for your loan

LendingTree.com

Corporate HQ: Charlotte, North Carolina

NO CHARGE   CALC.   QUOTES   ARCHIVE

E-COM

LendingTree.com uses the reverse auction format. You can apply for a loan in one of the major categories, and then LendingTree will offer your application (devoid of identifying information, such as your name or social security number) to its body of more than 100 lending institutions. Within one day, interested lenders will return bids to you. LendingTree is also a delectable site for people who like calculators. There are dozens of them, including one entitled, "How Long Should I Keep a Car?" In many cases, as that calculator shows, it costs more to keep one car for 10 years than to buy four new ones in the same span. (And that is what makes America great.)

just one more thing . . .

Interest.com
Mortgage Market Information Services

Corporate HQ: Chicago, Illinois

NO CHARGE   CALC.

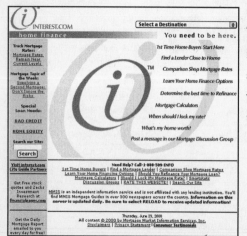

One of the humbling aspects of taking out a loan is accepting that your timing may be inadvertently brilliant or abysmal, regarding shifting interest rates. To understand that aspect of credit, whether or not you ever learn to beat it, look at the page on Interest.com called When Should I Lock in My Rate? Its discussion of interest-rate moves, updated every weekday, explains which events have affected the rates, and how. It also lists those events, such as Treasury auctions and new home sales reports, on a calendar for the current or upcoming week. Follow Interest.com's analyses for a period of several months, so that you can see where your little shell of a home or car purchase may ride on the ocean waves called interest rates.

Credit

The Long and Short of

* Obtain a copy of your credit report every two or three years and check it over.

* Married people should be especially careful to correct any mistakes or omissions which could compromise the future credit-worthiness of either individual.

* Whenever you are forced to miss payments for any loan or credit card, contact your creditor as soon as possible. You will generate much more cooperation and even patience by communicating honestly, than by slinking around in silence.

* Credit counseling services can help you to organize your finances, however bleak matters have become. In addition, they can intercede with your creditors and sometimes make arrangements that will allay drastic problems (i.e. evictions and repossessions).

* Having the right type of credit card for your current spending habits can save you substantial amounts of money in fees and unnecessary finance charges.

* Preparation is one of the most important factors in making a successful loan application; it may be the most important one. The more the lender knows about you and your plans, the more advantageously a loan can be structured.

Employment:
the world of opportunity

The Internet is a source for millions of job listings, but then, only one job is going to be the next job. To make sure it is a good one, you have to steer your career, a skill that can be learned. All the search engines in the world can't tell you what to do next, until you know what it is yourself.

Some people are always searching for a better job. Between job searches, you might catch them actually working. For them, the Internet is like a digital version of a horse-racing program, by which they can see how they're doing in the stampede. The web does make it possible to enrich your understanding of the employment market-place, which is a good idea even for those happily ensconced with one company. Visiting the steps below on a regular basis will let you see the trends and nuances of the job world as they unfold. In fact, this chapter is intended as much for the employed person as it is for the job seeker. Both must look out for themselves, and they can do so very effectively simply by staying abreast of the job market and its changing patterns.

step one: who do you think you are?
The job market has all sorts of hidden nooks and crannies, but then . . . so do you

Working at a job can either be a pleasure that makes the day fly by or an agony of excruciating boredom. Because of that peculiar law of physics, proven personally by most working people, it is a shame to spend even three seconds (or was it three years) in the wrong job. The sites in this step help you to constructively poke around among your own predilections and discover the type of work that will inspire your days, and still jibe with your long-range plans.

Insiders' Tour of Yahoo!—Careers
(careers.yahoo.com)

If you are thinking about a career change, Yahoo! Careers provides job descriptions as well as the industry outlook in almost a 100 different parts of the economy. Company Profiles, produced by WetFeet.com, provide extensive information culled from employees of approximately 50 major companies. Theses profiles include features such as What's Great/What's to Hate, candid views of the industry in question, and Real People, interviews with those already working in the field.

TIP: If you like what you read in one of the profiled companies, the Recruiting button provides complete contact information.

At Yahoo! Careers, job seekers can also browse through more than a million job postings. Or try a dream job on for size by entering the quarterly Fantasy Careers contest. Job seekers looking for visibility with employers can place a resume online, track the number of employers that view the resume, then sit back and wait for the employers to contact them.

To learn more about a successful job search, the Job Hunting Advice by careerjournal.com describes the most effective way to do anything, from writing a resume to impressing an interviewer. The Career Track section offers advice aimed at specific groups, such as high tech job seekers, immigrants, veterans, and entrepreneurs.

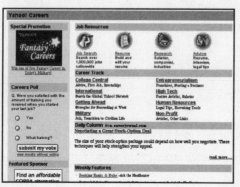

TIP: Under Research, Yahoo! Careers provides a wide array of sample cover letters and resumes.

NO CHARGE

SEARCH

quizzing your future

The Princeton Review, a company unaffiliated with a certain orange-and-black striped university in New Jersey, prepares students for SATs and other standardized tests. Its website has an even loftier goal: preparing students for life, that quintessential standardized test. The core of the site is the Princeton Review Quiz, which is intended to match personalities to suitable professions. The quiz is composed of 24 dandy questions, such as, "Would you rather be an auditor or a musician?" The assumption, of course, is that you can somehow make a choice between the two. A whole battery of such questions results in a list of jobs right for you: not necessarily auditor *or* musician, but ones with some subtle relationship to your predilections. I answered the questions faithfully, and the site produced a long list of possible jobs, one of which was none other than career counselor. I took that as a profound compliment, considering the source. The site includes other career advice, all cheerfully rendered, and descriptions of every job type on its lists.

REVIEW.com

Princeton Review

Corporate HQ: New York City, New York

NO CHARGE CALC. E-COM

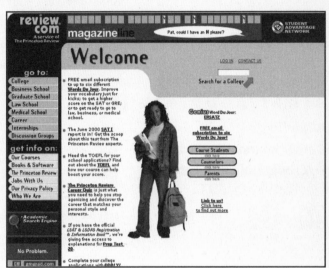

working for the job-seeker

Monster.com boasts that it will veritably cater your career, soup to nuts—or "intern to CEO," in its own estimation. The site currently has listings for about 300,000 jobs, but the job-search tool is effectively drowned out by the cacophony of job talk emanating on Monster.com. There are departments for updates on trends in specific sectors and for interviews with job-holders; chat rooms, advice columns, and a potent resume-preparation tool. While you shouldn't be dissuaded from using the job search when you need it, peruse the site just to gather momentum.

monster.com

TMP Worldwide

Corporate HQ: Maynard, Massachusetts, and Indianapolis, Indiana

NO CHARGE SEARCH

step two: know more than they do

Find out all about the companies, the industries, and the world that awaits you

After you know the kind of job you want, it is equally important to select a company upon which to bestow your efforts. The sites in this step will turn your attention outward toward the landscape of American industries and companies, so that you can see what sorts of firms are hiring what sorts of people. Even if you have no intention of leaving your current job, these sites can apprise you of your general worth in the marketplace, enabling you to negotiate accordingly with your employers. Or quit in a huff on Monday, should you learn that you are underpaid.

other people's jobs

ACInet.org
Career Information Net, the
U.S. Department of Labor
HQ: Washington, D.C.

NO CHARGE

SEARCH

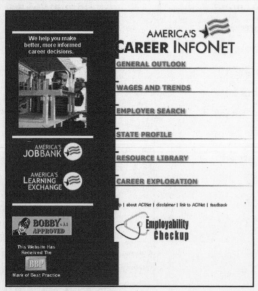

ACInet.org is a gold-medal site, endlessly interesting, either for the job seeker or the hopelessly nosy. Many people are in the former category—but everybody is in the latter, and so if you are curious as to what other people earn, the Wages and Trends page can discuss that subject from any angle. It has statistical trends by state and by occupation, but more pointedly, it has specific information for hundreds of job titles. For each job, there is a good description of the daily work, along with the median salary, nationally or by state, and the outlook. Randomly choosing the category Farm, Fishing, and Forestry, and specifying Idaho, for example, I was given a further choice of jobs, and selected Fallers and Buckers. The description explained what on earth that means (a person who fells trees and/or saws them), and the chart illustrated that nationally a faller makes $22,500, but in Idaho: $35,900. Apparently, Idaho is the place for fallers, in case you know any.

If you are more than just nosy and are actually seeking a job, ACInet.org will give you the latest data on the following, nationally or by state, and for any education level: fastest growing occupations; occupations with the most openings at the moment, and highest paying occupations. Nationally, the number one jobs in each of those categories were, at this writing: computer engineer, cashier, and surgeon (at a median of $124,800). Furthermore, the site will find employers of a certain type in any locale you want, a list not limited to companies that have openings at the moment. For example, I searched for airplane companies in Central Arkansas and was given a choice of towns, from which I selected Searcy, and the site gave complete information for four airplane companies (at least one was a crop-duster).

ACInet.org does not have specific job listings, but is connected with AJB.org, a major source of employment notices.

Short shots

RileyGuide.com

gilt-edge employers

Famous for the "*Fortune* 500" ranking of the largest companies in America, *Fortune* magazine now has a whole list of lists, including two of interest to job hunters. One is the Most Admired Companies in the country and the other is the 100 Best Companies to work for. Either list can be enlightening, not necessarily so much for the companies that make the grade, but for the criteria you can borrow and use to evaluate potential employers for yourself. Both lists are available on *Fortune*'s web page, which is otherwise devoted to general corporate news. In the case of the best companies to work for, *Fortune* made its selection on the basis of perks, management attitude, and atmosphere in the workplace, among other factors.

fortune.com
Fortune **Magazine**
Corporate HQ: New York City, New York

NO CHARGE   ARCHIVE

corporate postings

The *Business Week* careers page offers articles both timely and archival on all aspects of working, with more emphasis than other sites on human resources issues, or matters of concern after you've been hired. The site has a unique job finder, in that it allows you to choose a company and see its current openings. If you have your heart set on working at Turtle Wax, for example, you can see its particular postings at BusinessWeek.com. Otherwise, you can specify an occupation and see general postings.

BusinessWeek.com/careers
Business Week **magazine**
Corporate HQ: New York City, New York

NO CHARGE   SEARCH   ARCHIVE

step three: finding a comfortable position

There are more than a million job postings on the Internet

Yahoo! quote:

Money can't buy friends, but you do get a better class of enemies.

—Spike Milligan,
quoted at 6FigureJobs.com

Along with Monster.com (listed in Step One), the sites in this step can help you find an opening and apply for it. While many people today consider relocation as a matter of no consequence, it is possible on each of these sites to specify a region or metropolitan area. That is, don't be intimidated by the sheer extent of the listings on the Internet. Don't be overconfident because of them, either. Your next job is to find your next job.

employment section

CareerPath.com
Corporate HQ: Los Angeles, California

NO CHARGE   SEARCH

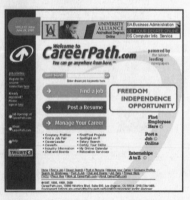

The nation's largest newspaper chains decided early on to fight the effect of the Internet by joining it. Like Cars.com (see *Automobiles*), CareerPath.com represents a consortium of more than 100 daily newspapers around the country; it makes all of the employment ads in each one available on the Internet, to be searched by geography, job-title, or keyword. Or even by newspaper, if that matters much to a job-hunter. CareerPath.com goes beyond the newsprint, however, and also pulls postings from company sites all over the web. The resulting list includes more than 330,000 openings, none of which remain on the site for more than two weeks. Skimming through the job-titles on the search tool, I was virtually ignited to see the word, "playwright." I thought Broadway was beckoning at last, but alas and alack, as Shakespeare might say, out of 330,889 listings, nobody wanted a playwright that day.

job service

AJB.org
America's Job Bank
U.S. Department of Labor and the Public Employment Service
HQ: Washington D.C.

NO CHARGE   SEARCH

The Job Bank has close to 1.5 million jobs on file, though not one call for a playwright, it is true. But, otherwise, the jobs range widely: from an acquisitions editor in Albany, New York at $65,000 per annum to a blackjack dealer in Las Vegas, at $5.35 per hour, to name but two out of the whole kettle.

AJB.org is not only trying to help with your next job, but with your next one after that, and so there is a link to ALX.org, the American Learning Exchange, which provides advice and leads on training courses for job enrichment.

NO CHARGE   SEARCH

In this kaleidoscope of a modern civilization, there is no reason to work nine-to-five at what they call "a real job." Not when some people will pay you to play: The trick is finding those people, that's all. CoolJobs.com has 75,000 of them. As it says in its memo to employers, "If you are looking for a C++ programmer, a furniture salesperson or an administrative assistant, this is not the right site for you."

And so, if your answer to the question on Review.com, "Would you prefer to be an auditor or a musician?" is *I'd rather be a salmon fishing guide in Alaska,* then you will feel quite at home on CoolJobs.com. Two of the recent job postings on the site were for a general manager for a baseball team on the Carolina coast, and for a dancer in the Cirque de Soleil show.

And they call those *jobs*. Ha!

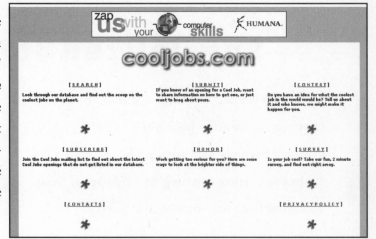

NO CHARGE   SEARCH

You aren't reading this chapter because you want to do something nice for someone else, are you? To be crass, then, volunteering is a good career move. You can usually land a volunteer job for which you have absolutely no credentials and no experience, perhaps only some welcome enthusiasm. If you can prove yourself a success in a volunteer job, though, it can prove to potential employers that you have skills that are worth real money. Volunteer-Match.com allows you to search for openings near your home, but it also lists opportunities for telecommuting tasks that can be rendered at your convenience, from your own computer.

Why be crass about it, though? People in trouble, animals, the land and water: They need you. They just can't pay in money, only in other things, including experience.

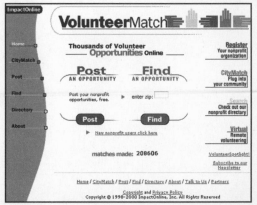

Specialized Job Sites

Some are organized according to WHAT you do . . .

Imcor.com—executive positions

6FigureJobs.com—high-paying jobs

TJobs.com—telecommuting, in a number of fields

YorkshirePlace.com—insurance industry

Some are organized according to WHO you are . . .

BlackCollegian.com—graduates of color

NewMobility.com—disabled

Saludos.com—English-speaking Hispanics

VetJobs—military veterans

Employment

The Long and Short of

* Have long-term goals and don't lose sight of them.

* Don't rely on your company and those within it for industry news. Stay aware of trends and opportunities through competitors' publications or websites, or through professional organizations.

* Continue to maintain your resume even when you are happily employed; it will force you to assess your career as others see it.

* Spend more time researching jobs than applying for them. That is, sending a well-prepared letter and resume for just the right job is generally much more effective than a mass mailing.

Insurance:

a piece of mind

Your house is no more solid than the insurance policy that will rebuild it in the event of a disaster. Your car is no faster than the coverage that will replace it in case of an accident, and so it is the same with other types of insurance. Coverage is never "one size fits all." It must be equal to the life you know.

In this chapter, we try to lead you through a virtual meeting with an insurance agent: finding out what your needs are; inquiring into the all-important area of health coverage, and seeing about the actual cost of good coverage. We have tried to steer you toward sites that give a ballpark quote without compromising your privacy—or at least without asking your name. Many insurance sites insist that you tell them who you are and where you can be bothered—that is, *contacted*. It's not just a ploy. Many forms of coverage really are more prudently purchased through the course of discussion with a professional. But it is also true that many websites generate revenue by selling leads to insurance agents. This section gives a distinct priority to sites that allow you to gather information without being seen.

step one: determining your needs

Websites can liven up the process of tailoring coverage to fit the shape of your life

The variables associated with insurance are myriad. Chief among them is the basic policy, itself—not only do companies write many different types of coverage within any one category, but they also individualize certain clauses. The sites in this step help to prepare you for the choices you will have to make within any insurance policy. You may not need to look further than the first site, Insure.com, which offers a profusion of insurance news and advice, though the other sites are strong in specific areas as well.

Insiders' Tour of Yahoo!—Insurance
(insurance.yahoo.com)

You can obtain free quotes and in-depth advice for many different kinds of insurance at Yahoo! Finance, including life and health, home and renter's, and auto. For example, under the topic of Auto Insurance, you can use an analyzer tool to make sure you are looking for the right amount of coverage. You can also take a Savings Quiz to determine if there are any ways to cut your auto insurance premiums. Completing the process, you can ask for a custom quote, tailored to your vehicle and driving habits.

TIP: Familiarize yourself with the automobile claim-filing tips before you need to file a claim.

Other sections are just as helpful. On the Life and Health page of Yahoo!! Finance, quotes for basic term life insurance are readily available. There are also answers to frequently asked questions regarding all types of life insurance, and a collection of informative articles, including one that describes the differences between term and whole-life insurance. The Health Plan analyzer will help ascertain your medical coverage needs, and quotes are available for all types. The Home and Renter's Insurance page also provides information on reducing premiums, along with quotes.

TIP: If you own a computer, look at the article about how to insure a PC.

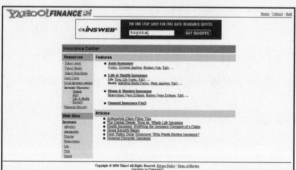

NO CHARGE   CALC.   QUOTES

NO CHARGE   CALC.   ARCHIVE

Insure.com does not exactly sell insurance, but it is as complete a site as there is for learning about policies, companies, and you. Founded by a journalist, it is noticeably well-edited, with original articles in a newspaper format. And few insurance-related websites are as objective: Insure.com generates original investigative reports, focusing on specific practices and companies. The site will also help you to form your own investigative report on any insurance companies to which you may trust your future. In conjunction with Standard & Poor's, the site lets you check the financial ratings of insurers, based on their ability to fulfill claims under even disastrous conditions.

The Complaint Finder goes beyond a company's mere ability to pay a claim, and helps assess its willingness to do so. Using state-supplied files, Insure.com lists companies according to the number of complaints that were upheld in arbitration. Not all states are covered (not all of them keep such records), but the Complaint Finder can be a compelling tool: If you look at a list of HMOs doing business in New York State in 1997 for example, and note that one has a grand total of zero upheld complaints and one, albeit a larger company, has 742 corroborated complaints, it starts you thinking. Either company A has the most docile clientele ever assembled, or it is a pretty straight-shooting outfit. Adjunct to the Complaint Finder is Insure.com's Lawsuit Library, through which you can peek into the legal scrapes faced by any one company.

Insure.com has pages explaining the nuances of major types of insurance, but for those getting ready to buy a policy, it is worth a visit to the state-by-state insurance advisory. Along with outlines of specific requirements, it offers sample rates for different types of drivers. If you feel ready to request an actual quote, Insure.com has links with a handful of sites operated by various sellers.

insurance tutorial with wit

RelianceDirect.com
Corporate HQ: Valley Forge,
Pennsylvania

RelianceDirect deserves an award for making its tutorial on insurance so amusing and yet so clear that anyone can benefit from it. The site is especially strong in explaining automobile insurance, though it covers all types of policies. At the core is the English-Insurance/Insurance-English Dictionary. It is not in dictionary form at all, but is laid out as a chart illustrating the components of auto insurance. The explanation of a Property Damage Liability is "This covers any damage your vehicle may cause to somebody else's car, house, fishery, etc."

Despite the occasional head-on collision with a fishery, no site covers the basics of insurance in a more conducive way than RelianceDirect.

up close to your insurance needs

LIFE-line.org
Life and Health Insurance
Foundation for Education

LIFE—or "LahIFfE" as the anti-acronym league might put it—is a trade group for the insurance industry. The investigative material on this site is scant, though if there were any, it would undoubtedly uncover the dark path to those who advocate government-sponsored health insurance. (LIFE-line is biased against it.) Politics aside, however (and it is a shame from either perspective that healthcare *is* politics), LIFE-line.org offers short primers on several types of major insurance. Its most valuable tool is the one with the eeriest name: the Human Life Value Calculator.

The Human Life Value Calculator (sounding like a built-in appliance at Frankenstein's castle) determines the income you would earn through to retirement. It determines the lump sum necessary to produce your lost income for the sake of your family, calculating the means to do so through the site's Insurance Needs Calculator. These figures will help you to construct a life insurance policy suitable to your needs.

Those people who forego medical coverage, thinking themselves stoical, thrifty, or just lucky, ought to look at the Cost of Care Estimator in the Health Insurance primer. It is fun to use, as you look at two otherwise healthy-looking people, and click on 22 common ailments hovering all around them, to see what the repair bills would run. Youch!

Another industry trade group, the Insurance Information Institute, maintains a site that carries a steady flow of news and advice. While not the most pointed or insightful place to start your insurance assessment, it is a good stop to make along the way. The topics listed under Individuals' Questions offer some offbeat ideas, under headings such as Insurance for Twentysomethings.

You don't always know what you don't know, especially when it comes to insurance. The LCGroup site fills in the smaller gaps important to individualizing coverage. On its site, the Glossary, is much more than a list of definitions. It is a notebook of information related to specific situations. For example, "Important Information Regarding Leased Vehicles," (under L), explains how some automobile policies fall painfully short of lessors' replacement clauses. Most insurance agents can keep you informed of such details in assembling strong coverage, but if you plan on bypassing agents as much as possible, by finding and buying policies online, it behooves you to peruse the notes found on III.org and LCGroup.com.

LCGroup also provides a simple way to test the waters for term-life insurance. Unlike many other sites, it does not require you to register or tell your name and e-mail address in order to request an initial quote. With seven questions, it will immediately give you a list of insurance companies and their quotes, leaving the next move up to you.

general news

III.org
Insurance Information Institute
HQ: New York City, New York

NO CHARGE   CALC.   ARCHIVE

specific tips

LCGroup.com
Lewis-Chester Group
Corporate HQ: Summit, New Jersey

NO CHARGE   E-COM

step two: in sickness or in health

Coverage for medical expenses is a personal responsibility

Short shots

HIAA.org—health insurance information from industry trade group

Weissratings.com—rankings on the worst insurance companies

Healthcare is now the largest industry in the nation. Meanwhile, the scramble to pay for it has become our roughest indoor sport. All sorts of logical options are open to you, except one, which is no coverage at all. Should you require expensive medical treatment without having any coverage, then everyone who cares for you will be financially ruined trying to pay your way. The two sites in this step explain the many types of healthcare coverage available, first through private insurers and then through Federal programs.

exploring private coverage

HealthAxis.com

Corporate HQ: East Norriton, Pennsylvania

NO CHARGE   QUOTES   E-COM

HealthAxis specializes in health coverage, representing seven companies ready to sell policies in most states. Two aspects of the site, though, are especially helpful no matter where you ultimately buy a policy. The Profiles included in the Advisor section reflect 14 typical situations and discuss the coverage bestsuited to each. Among them are, for example, "Entrepreneurs," or "Recently Divorced." The profiles are intended to point you toward a purchase on the site, but, nonetheless, they provide ideas that may just cover your needs. Tools and Help includes a chart comparing two sample health policies. Whatever the point being made with the two samples on the page, the chart itself is a very good structure by which to evaluate any medical policy. It lists 30 facts that you should know in advance about your coverage—print it out or just note the details as you go about acquiring the coverage you need.

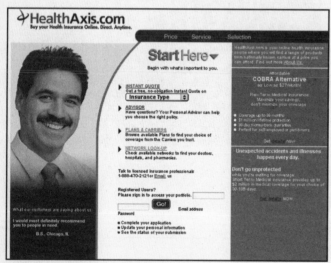

HealthAxis's Instant Quote tool allows you to request four or five preliminary quotes, with options detailed.

HCFA covers 39 million Americans, most of them older, through its Medicare program and 36 million needy Americans through Medicaid. Its sprightly site provides details about both programs. One tool that Medicare recipients will find especially useful is Medicare Compare. First, it locates qualified plans in your area; both privately issued ones and the standard Medicaid coverage. Once you have chosen two of them, Medicare Compare will line them up side-by-side, with data on cost, benefits, and care. The chart lays out just what you will pay, what you get and, moreover, what other people in the particular program have gotten in terms of service.

HCFA.gov
Health Care Financing
Administration
HQ: Washington, D.C.

NO CHARGE

step three: buying a policy online
Once you know what you need, the Internet provides sources for coverage

There are two ways to buy insurance online. The first is to bring a dimensional understanding of the policy you need and to order it through the web. The second, appropriate for those who mainly just want a lower premium, is to match your current policy in every respect and to request quotes. The two sites in this step offer different ways to approach companies, or to let them approach you, as the case may be.

Insweb.com
Corporate HQ: Redwood City, California

NO CHARGE   CALC.   QUOTES   ARCHIVE

E-COM

Through 49 participating companies, Insweb.com offers many types of policies: auto, health, homeowners, renters, term life, whole life, and even pet insurance. Should you want to price an actual policy, Insweb has you register and send an application online. The first quotes based on that application will start arriving in your personal QuotePad within 15 minutes; others may take days to arrive. You can then contact the

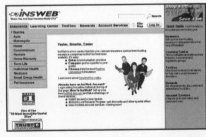

companies of your choice for further details. You will be buying the policy directly from them, not Insweb.

naming a price

Ebix.com
Corporate HQ: Atlanta, Georgia

NO CHARGE

QUOTES

E-COM

Ebix is a growing computer service company with origins in insurance. In the Ebix system, you don't get a quote—you give one. The company lets you describe the policy you want, in the areas of auto, home, health, and life. According to one of the Internet's favorite pricing mazurkas, you then state the price you are ready to pay. Insurance agents will examine your figure and contact you with offers that match or better it.

just one more thing . . .

BadFaithInsurance.org
InsuranceFraud.org

NO CHARGE

ARCHIVE

The insurance company that accepts your premiums, year in and year out, and then refuses to pay a legitimate claim when times are dire, commits a betrayal of the worst kind. BadFaithInsurance.org rates well known insurance companies on their record of paying claims. The site also lists lawyers who specialize in claims cases. The only betrayal as bitter as a company that does not pay legitimate claims is the customer who collects on illegitimate ones. The Coalition Against Insurance Fraud, at InsuranceFraud.org, cites the worst fraud cases of the week, while tracing the effect of such fakery on other premiums. As these two sites make clear, the insurance industry for all its gleaming skyscrapers, is balanced on a pinpoint of trust.

Link List

GetInfo.com-Click Resources.
Insurance-Finance.com
Wisc.edu/insure/resource.
htm

Insurance

* Which do you suppose is worse: to be under-insured, leaving yourself vulnerable, or to be over-insured, and paying for coverage that you simply don't need? Think about it, because both are very common occurrences.

* Another pathetic situation is also quite common: to be under-insured in some vital respects, and to be, nonetheless, over-insured in areas quite irrelevant to your status. Understand your policy and what you are paying for, and update your policies every two or three years.

* To enable yourself to afford healthcare insurance, covering catastrophic problems in particular, specify a high deductible.

* Before accepting a policy with any company, investigate its financial standing and its track record for paying claims.

Real estate: reeling in realtors

This chapter not only guides you through the rather giddy process of selecting a house online, it includes the rather more sobering processes of transacting real estate, financing it, and making you actually need it.

Moving, as my aunt once said, is hell. Then she kept using it in a sentence; "It came like a bat out of *moving*." It was very funny, which is more than anyone can say about moving. The Internet, however, is providing a fresh place to start the process, by turning every home computer into a multiple-listing service, lined with descriptions of millions and millions of homes. In the face of such ease, it is hard to recollect how people selected homes in the olden days of four or five years ago and without the Internet: especially homes in distant locales. Did they actually have to go to the new locale before they picked out a house? Did they go in a horse and buggy? It's difficult to recall, at present, when the simplest of searches brings up gaggles of homes for sale, in picture and description. The use of action-video virtual tours has tempted some people to buy a house in just two steps: point and click. Stop short of that new trend—virtual tours carry all the journalistic integrity of postcards from the beach. They won't show the cesspool next door, or anything else you might not like.

The steps below round out a list of the most attractive browsing sites on the web, but they also walk you through some of the more daunting aspects of home buying, including trying mortgages on for size, so that you can be both enthusiastic *and* realistic about the new home you choose.

Insiders' Tour of Yahoo!—Real Estate
(realestate.yahoo.com)

If you are looking for a new place to live, Yahoo! Real Estate offers more than one million home listings that are easily searched, either by community or by type of residence. In addition, the site offers information to address the many concerns surrounding a home purchase, such as the impact of property taxes. The array of calculators, mortgage quotes, and prequalification services available can also save you money. For those who are thinking of selling, the site offers an estimate of home values, according to neighborhood, and even lets you list your home for sale for free. Yahoo! Real Estate also lists rental properties, including both apartments and single family homes.

TIP: Whether you want to find a roommate or to be a roommate, you can post a notice at Yahoo! Real Estate.

For anyone who is facing a move, the site offers many informational tools to research schools, find child care, and learn about cities. You can compare almost any two cities in the country, seeing at a glance how they match up in a variety of topics, including employment, taxes, crime, and weather.

TIP: If you are especially interested in any of the comparison topics, click it to see a ranking of all the cities, best to worst.

And once you have your ideal location, Yahoo! Real Estate also has a section devoted to remodeling, where you can locate an architect, designer, or contractor in your area. There is also advice on how to plan and execute a home improvement project successfully.

NO CHARGE   SEARCH   CALC.

step one: home work
Evaluating the place you're in now and the options you have

Long before you shuffle through your first open house, you should understand the way that the home buying process is likely to unfold. Each of the sites in this step offers advance preparation. The first, CSWonline.com, is included for those who already own a home. HomePath.com and HUD.com represent two organizations, Fannie Mae and the Department of Housing and Urban Development, that have done more than any other two institutions in America to help people who want to own a home. They can help you, too.

home valuation

CSWonline.com
Case, Shiller, Weiss
Corporate HQ: Cambridge, Massachusetts

With so many people buying or selling homes in the paperless—but not wallpaperless—world of online real estate, CSW offers a suitably digital means of determining the current worth of nearly any home in the United States. The Characteristics and Sales Analysis tool on the site is an evaluation service based on the company's property records database. Using algorithms and other mathematical manipulations, CSW can supply an estimated value for any piece of property in under 10 minutes.

While many real estate agents will stop by to give you a free estimate of your home's selling price, their judgment can easily be slanted: toward a high price in order to please you, or toward a low one, so that they can unload the old shack quickly, should you decide to list it. A professional real estate appraiser will give you a much more objective price estimate, though the cost is likely to run into several hundred dollars. It is generally well worth the cost, arming you not only with a viable market price, but with all kinds of information regarding your house and neighborhood—things you'll probably wish you'd known before you moved in. However, it is not necessary in every case to make the expenditure for a professional estimate. For that reason, the CSWonline.com service is a reasonable alternative. The only information required is the address, the last known value of the property—and the number of your credit card (the service costs $35).

Good Buys in Renting

The prevailing pressure from the workplace and the family—and the government—is to own your home and to do so as soon as possible. In some sociological sense, the homeowner is perceived, *de facto,* as a solid citizen. Yet in the financial sense, home ownership can prove to be imprudent. A few of the situations that encourage renting, even for those who can well afford a downpayment:

* **The serious investor.** While a home purchase is certainly a valid means of diversifying your overall portfolio as a return on investment, it may not keep up with your other holdings. For example, home prices in your area may be traditionally flat, while your return in the markets may be 10 or 15 percent per year. People in this category should certainly invest accordingly—with safety of principal as a high priority.

* **The long-term borrower.** If home prices are flat in your area and you have no intention of committing the resources to paying off the mortgage as soon as possible, you may well find that you lose money when selling. Those forced to sell at the price they paid will lose money on the overall transaction, because their mortgage payments have been paid only to service the interest, not to pay down the principal. As for those selling at below the price they paid, they will not only lose money on paper, but may have to write a check, when the selling price does not cover the remainder of their own mortgage. Unless you are firmly planning 1) to stay in a home for a long time, 2) pay the mortgage with alacrity, or 3) to sell the house for substantially more than you paid, renting may cost you less than home ownership.

* **Risk reducers.** Many people consider that home ownership is a form of security when times are bad, and it may be, especially if the home is owned outright. Yet when times are bad, either for the homeowner or for the community at large, home ownership can become a liability. The renter, in this case, has the greater security, assuming that his or her extra money has been deposited safely. Even in buoyantly good times, you may be persuaded to reduce your overall risk by renting, simply because you are already grappling with other risky or sensitive situations in your life, such as the ill-health of a family member, or your being in a high-risk employment situation, such as starting a new company.

The aforementioned are some of the considerations that should make you stop, think, and calculate with your own situation in mind. While home ownership is right for most people, that certainly doesn't make it right for you. Note: If you do rent, rather than buy, have the discipline to *save* the difference in payments and expenses, placing it in a responsible investment.

advice on the home-buying process

Fannie Mae originated in 1938 as a federally sponsored source for mortgages. Thirty years later, in 1968, it cut itself free from the government, becoming a private corporation, and today, it looms as the largest backer of home mortgages in the country: One in four homes now carries a Fannie Mae mortgage. For all its prosperity, the company retains its aura of public service, and its website is steeped in common sense. The three tutorials on the site, called "paths," contain self-tests within the text, to customize points as they are made. The HomeStarter Path, for example, directs you to a calculator on How Much House Can You Afford? That is not a rare item on a homebuyer's site, but Fannie Mae does a better job than most in explaining the import of such figures. Because no website can answer every question pertinent to every region and person, Fannie Mae's site can also direct you to a mortgage counselor, most of whom are affiliated with non-profit agencies.

HomePath.com
Fannie Mae
Corporate HQ Washington, D.C.

 NO CHARGE CALC. ARCHIVE

home-buying for all

The Federal government's Department of Housing and Urban Development uses its site to empower all Americans to reach the long-cherished dream of home ownership. No wonder it is such an extensive site. For those who don't have much money, HUD maintains a listing of funds and special loans. There is specific advice on programs for farmworkers, the disabled, the homeless, and others sometimes ignored in the dream of real estate ownership. The site is also directed at a much more common group, one that has included at one time or another every homeowner, rich or poor—the first-time buyer. Among other programs offered through the site is

HUD.gov
HQ: Washington, D.C.

 NO CHARGE SEARCH

HUD's own bridal registry, which allows newly-weds to accumulate mortgage money, instead of more knickknacks for the apartment. If you are looking to buy property, the Homebuying page offers links to an array of agencies with houses to sell. Included among them are the IRS, Fannie Mae, and the FDIC.

step two: open house
You can search through certain neighborhoods or whole countries

The goal of this step probably ought to be obvious: to help you narrow your choice in a new home down to one swell dream house, all in mere minutes, if not seconds. That would be entirely possible, using the sites below, but it is certainly not the motivation of Step Two. There is no reason to narrow your choice in real estate. This step hopes, on the contrary, to broaden your first inclination in housing into a dozen separate ideas, each of which takes hold of your imagination, at least for a little while. For that reason, nearly every site below reflects a different type of home, or a distinctive way to look for them.

the most homes on the web

Realtor.com
Corporate HQ: Washington, D.C.

NO CHARGE

SEARCH

CALC.

QUOTES

Early in 1999, an independent auditing group called Clareity checked the accuracy of the claims made by various home-listing agencies on the Internet. Websites that claimed to represent as many as 700,000 homes turned out, in fact, to offer only half that number or even less. However, the results showed that the site making the very biggest claim, Realtor.com, at 1.3 million listings, was the most truthful, to boot: 1.2 million listings were counted at the time of the audit. If 1.2 million homes present enough of a choice for you—for some people it would represent only the first Sunday afternoon's worth of looking—then Realtor.com is an organized site at which to browse the possibilities. House-hunting is a matter of six clicks.

After designating a state, then a region, then a town (or neighborhood), you list the type of dwelling that is desired, along with the number of bedrooms/bathrooms, square footage, and the price range. Usually, a wide choice results. Operated by the National Association of Realtors, with its 720,000 members, Realtor.com is the flagship of the Homestore.com family of websites.

wide-angle searches

Homes.com
Corporate HQ: Menlo Park, California

NO CHARGE · CALC. · QUOTES · ARCHIVE

Homes.com features a home finder not unlike that of Realtor.com, except it allows for some welcome flexibility in the choice of location. If you are one of those people that *has* to live in Beverly Hills, and that doesn't mean Bel-Air, then you can direct Homes.com to be just that specific. However, at your direction, it can also include for your consideration homes that are within either 5 or 15 miles of your designated town. That is particularly helpful for people who are relocating to areas that they don't happen to know, village by village. Search for Jamesville, New York, for example, and with a little flexibility, you can also see homes in beautiful downtown Southwood. Only the *cogniscenti*, Homes.com, and a couple of dozen cows know that Southwood is practically Jamesville and vice versa.

private sales

Owners.com
Corporate HQ: San Francisco, California

NO CHARGE · CALC. · QUOTES

An FSBO, in the parlance of the trade, is a home that is on the market without the services of a real estate agent, "For Sale by Owner." About 200,000 FSBO's are listed on Owners.com, though for those browsing for a new home, an FBSO is almost indistinguishable from an FSWR, or a "For Sale With Realtor," to coin a new term.

Owners.com is especially helpful for those selling their own homes, guiding self-sufficient homeowners all the way through the process of handling their own transaction. Sellers are charged for listings at three levels, ranging from a free listing with one picture, to

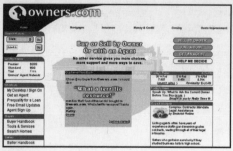

a $289-package that includes a virtual tour of the house being sold. If the home does not sell through one of the priced packages, but later does sell through a real estate agent, then the site provides a complete refund. Owners.com claims that, on average, its clients save $10,000 in commissions and fees using its system.

building plans

Homestyles.com
Corporate HQ: St. Paul, Minnesota

 NO CHARGE SEARCH QUOTES E-COM

Homestyles.com sells houses that don't yet exist except as a gleam in some customer's eye. The site is a storehouse for 8,300 building plans, which can be purchased for prices starting at about $400 for a single set. To search for a new house, you need only denote your desired square footage, style (colonial, Spanish, etc.), number of floors, bedrooms, and baths. The resulting selection will include a sketch of the house and basic floorplans, with specs. After using other Internet home finders, it may feel odd not to denote a location for your new house. But then, that's just the point of Homestyles.com.

acreage

Land.net
Corporate HQ: Brooklyn, New York

 NO CHARGE SEARCH QUOTES

If you are looking for location (and nothing but), Land.net offers empty lots all the way around the world. Click on Greece and find 3 acres on an island overlooking the sea and a mountain range (I don't know how it could overlook both, but then that is the splendor of international sales talk). Click on Brazil and find 6,000 hectares worth of Amazon forest. Should that leave you wondering what the heck a hectare is, the site has a conversion tool that translates such metrics into English measurement—indicating that there are 14,826 acres of the Amazon rainforest out there, yours to save. If you need a slightly more conventional place to build a new home, though, Land.net offers open property in the United States and Canada. In addition to residential sites, it also lists commercial property, islands, and farmland.

Short Shots

LifeNet.com—charts explaining different types of mortgages, with many calculators
MoverQuotes.com—estimates from many moving companies

Another entry from the HomeStore.com family of websites, Springstreet is directed toward people looking for apartments. That being the case, it is a little hard to understand why the site recently changed its name from allapartments.com to the rather more obscure Springstreet.com. The site represents managed apartments, meaning multi-unit developments and large buildings. Little widows renting out an attic flat are not included. Nonetheless, the scope is impressive, covering more than 6,000 U.S. cities.

Springstreet.com
Corporate HQ: San Francisco, California

 NO CHARGE SEARCH QUOTES E-COM

step three: a mortgage in the right neighborhood

Before you even start looking for a house, determine the size and the features of the mortgage you can handle comfortably

The Credit chapter features several websites that describe mortgages and the interest rates that define them. Those sites represent, naturally enough, lenders. RealEstate.com, the sole website in Step Three, devotes considerable space to mortgages, but with more attention—perhaps even more sympathy—paid to the borrower's entire home-buying experience.

Link List

Mortgage Café—links to home-loan sites

RealEstate.com, holder of the most enviable domain name in the field, caters especially to real estate professionals, offering business-to-business news and networking. However, on the right side of the homepage, you will find a section devoted to Information for Homebuyers and Sellers. Click on the Calculators button, and you can use a dozen of the more incisive home-finance tools on the Internet. They are not necessarily complex, but they are well posed. The side-by-side comparison called "Which Loan Is Better?" for example, can point out the long-term benefits of even a fairly small difference in terms. It is simple to use, having only five blanks to be filled. As sobering, though a little more predictable, is the calculator called, "Which Is Better, 15 or 30 Years?" In reference to a mortgage, the answer is nearly always 15, but the degree to which the shorter term is better may be worth weighing against the background of other considerations, such as life as you know it.

RealEstate.com
www.realestate.com
Corporate HQ: Atlanta, Georgia

The centerpiece of RealEstate.com's offering to civilians is its Mortgage Auction, also found on the right side of the homepage. The online application covers three pages and asks for information related to, not surprisingly, the house you want, the money you have, and the money you need. Once the application is officially submitted, RealEstate.com will make it available to more than 320 approved lenders, though identifying information such as your name and social security number will be removed first. The lender submitting the best bid, in the form of the lowest percentage rate, will be awarded the right to contact you within 24 hours. You are under no obligation to accept the mortgage offered. However, assuming that your application was accurate, the lender is indeed obliged to grant the mortgage.

just one more thing . . .

ImproveNet.com
Corporate HQ: Redwood City, California

NO CHARGE　SEARCH　CALC.

Even after you have a house, there is still something you probably don't have. And that is someone to come and fix it. Or fix it up. Tradespeople are hard to enlist, probably owing to the fact that as a breed, they don't return telephone calls or keep appointments. ImproveNet.com uses the Internet to establish contact between clients and contractors, architects, or designers. According to the system, four of them—four!—will contact you after seeing your proposal for home improvements, as submitted online through the site. However, even if you do not avail yourself of the Find a Contractor/Architect/Designer pages, ImproveNet offers cyber-estimates for two of the most popular areas of improvement: kitchen and bathroom renovations. The very detailed calculators—the latter was given the nickname the "lavatory laboratory"— allow you to tinker with plans until you know the possibilities and costs well enough to open up a discussion with a contractor.

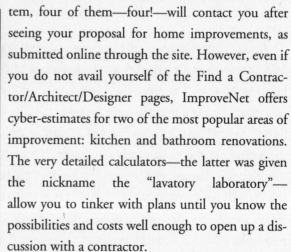

Real Estate

* Learn about all of the variations on mortgages—there are close to a dozen in common use.

* Pay as large a down payment as you can: Don't be tempted by lenders willing to extend a home loan on a minimum five percent down. Financing 95 percent of a home purchase is a strain on your long-term plans. Twenty percent is a far more realistic start, even if the minimum offered is less.

* If you can pay a higher premium and shorten the term of the mortgage, you will realize substantial savings in interest. Consider that well in advance of shopping for a home, so that you are not tempted to buy a more expensive home than is reasonable for your overall financial situation.

* Bi-weekly mortgage payments, rather than monthly ones, can make a significant difference in the amount of interest paid over the course of a mortgage.

* Many bargains are available through the auction market. Owners who care far more about expediency than profit very often turn to the auctioneer. While the houses are typically at the lower end of the scale, the cost can be little more than a song ($3,000-$5,000 is not uncommon). Some first class properties go through the auction, as well, but in any case, prices are usually below market.

Retirement planning and college savings: taking into account

Time is even better than money, when it comes to savings. Whether philosophically it is better than money overall is for you to decide. Financially, though, every way that you can find to let the days, months, and years sink deep down into your money will be rewarded.

By following the steps in this chapter, you can assess your position not in terms of money alone, but in terms of money in its relationship to time. The two are very often conjoined, but never more so than in the quiet growth of a retirement or college savings account. As the steps below illustrate—and as many an analyst has said before—patience can do most of the work of reaching a savings goal. That is where planning comes in. Don't look at it as a means of constraint that keeps you from spending your money freely. That is the discipline of planning, but the power of it lies in harnessing time to do as much of your work as possible.

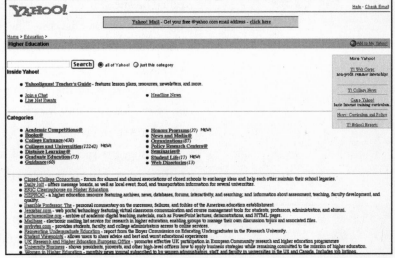

step one: it's never too late to start planning

It just costs more to do less, the longer you wait

The three sites included in this step offer interactive planning techniques. Though they vary in level of detail, they are each worthwhile. John Hancock's planning tool can be used in the space of about 20 minutes, while FPlanAuditors' planner may take several hours just to initiate it properly. Depending on your own approach to the subject, any of these sites can help you give shape to your financial future.

designing a custom plan

JHancock.com

Corporate HQ: Boston, Massachusetts

NO CHARGE

CALC.

E-COM

John Hancock's Portrait Planning tool does as its name suggests: paints a portrait of your financial situation, and then plans a means of attaining reasonable goals. While the planner is only one aspect of Hancock's website, which is otherwise concerned with the corporation's business, it is a popular online destination, offering an intermediate level of analysis. The crux of the planner is the Asset Allocation questionnaire, which makes one inquiry about your time horizon . . . and then eight about your stomach; that is, your tolerance for risk. With the resulting information, the planner suggests an asset allocation pie chart for you, showing by category just where your long-term savings would sit best. A second section of the allocation suggests specific mutual funds that would fit into the template. In case you are tempted to forego planning for now, the final chart on the Portrait Planner compares the projected five-year performance of your current portfolio and the one just tailored for you.

Hancock's Planning Silhouettes require less time, asking on average two simple questions, but making only basic forecasts. By noting your age and gender, one of them will give you an idea of a monthly premium for a long-term care policy covering your later years. Tell the College Planner that you have a ten-year-old who wants to go to an exclusive four-

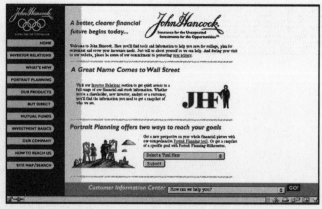

year school and it will let know that you should be saving $14,000 per year. Starting right after lunch.

understanding the priorities

The retirement calculator in USNews.com's News You Can Use section is a seven-step process. The first time I filled it out, it deciphered my information and then informed me how much money I will need for retirement—$41 million. "How will you get the money?" it then asked. I'd already been curious about that very fact. "The first place you might look is Social Security," it continued.

USNews.com
US News & World Reports
magazine
Corporate HQ: Washington, D.C.

NO CHARGE CALC.

The best thing about USNews.com's Retirement Calculator is not its dour wit, however unintended, but the inclusion of the Dig Deeper buttons throughout the planner. They not only indicate the many layers of construction within any proper financial plan, but explain them thoroughly, as well. The News You Can Use section also offers a tool to help select mutual funds, and a refinance calculator, along with other finders, such as the well-regarded Best Hospital Report, which ranks the top institutions in each of 16 specialties.

measuring your plans

The most comprehensive of the web's planning tools is the Plan Audit Wizard offered by FPlanAuditors. If you were to print out the financial plan that results from filling out the Wizard, the result would be a report at least 30 pages long, maybe 50. And even so, the site encourages you to complete and file several plans, for enrichment of your mind and perhaps your pocketbook. The pages peer into every aspect of your present and future, covering your proposed and actual holdings, retirement savings, intended withdrawals, expected benefits, tuition costs to be incurred (if any), and tax assumptions. To help you forecast the efficacy of your plan, FPlanAuditors' system applies historical analysis, telling you what *would have* happened to it, over any span during the past 70 years. This analysis has an effect something like a wind tunnel for the engineers—showing you where the interference will occur, under actual conditions.

FPlanAuditors.com
Financeware.com
Corporate HQ: Richmond, Virginia

NO CHARGE CALC.

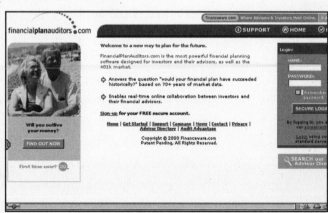

The site, which is very affable for all its serious intent, is free to use and has substantial benefits, if you are willing to invest the time. The FPlanAuditor is a trifle demanding for an amateur though. The company encourages people to work with an advisor—it certainly does so, having registered about 5,000 planners to use the website professionally, at a small cost.

Three Savings Techniques that Harness Time

* **Zero-coupon bond**—Buy a Zero-Coupon now for several thousand dollars and in 20 years, it will be worth exactly $20,000. The amount you pay upfront depends on the prevailing interest rate. Issued by the Treasury Department, the Zero-coupon (also known as the STRIP) bond does not generate interest payments during the life of the bond. Instead, all interest is compounded. Several financial houses issue equivalent bonds, which go by the acronyms TIGRs and CATS.

* **Index Funds**—In mutual funds, a fairly solid investment strategy is to make consistent purchases of Index Funds (representing market bellwethers such as the Dow Jones Industrial Average, the Wilshire 5000, or the S&P 500). Once you have determined a buying pattern, you must stick to it, through an index's peaks and valleys, in order to enjoy the benefit of averaging over time. Dividends should be reinvested in the fund. If you can, invest in two or three indices, on the same basis. While this index-averaging carries the risk of any equity (referring to shares that can drop in price), it has the benefit of relating your savings to markets which have traditionally out-performed, if nothing else, the rate of inflation.

* For long-term savings, buy your own certificates of deposit (CDs) or Treasuries, or leave your money in money market accounts. Mutual funds that are dedicated to these types of investments are sometimes tempting, for the convenience, and they are appropriate for those who may want to shift their money around. For long-term savings of 10 or more years, such mutual funds are less attractive. They may have the advantage of averaging many such purchases over time, to mitigate the chances of getting stuck with a relatively low-interest vehicle; however, in the long run, this advantage will nearly always be more than offset by the various management fees charged by the fund.

step two: the tunnel at the beginning of the light

Retirement savings accounts are far easier to create than ever before

In the realm of retirement planning, you are by no means on your own. Programs developed by the Federal government and many employers help you to extend your earning power, as it were, even to those years when you are no longer working. When Social Security started in 1935, it was designed simply to keep retirees from going hungry or homeless, both conditions having formerly been quite common for the elderly, even in prosperous times. Today, your plan should be much more ambitious.

In the perception of many people now employed, it is by no means enough that retirement income be adequate or even equivalent to a working salary: They want it to provide an even higher scale of living, with more travel and freedom of expenditure than before. And considering that retirement can easily account for a third of one's time on earth, it may as well be lush, if planning can make it so. The sites below focus on the strongest of the programs designed to play a part in your retirement.

Short Shots

Ebri.org—Employee Benefit Research Institute site; data on how your peers are using 401K and other plans
Pathfinder.com/ParentTime /work/home/—good tuition toolbox, and other financial notes for parents
http://research.aarp.org/ econ/—AARP site offering serious research and updates in retirement planning
Scholarships.SallieMae.com —well-connected search tool
Wiser.heinz.org—dedicated to helping women plan financially for retirement

your government account

SSA.gov
Social Security Administration
Corporate HQ: Washington, D.C.

NO CHARGE

CALC.

ARCHIVE

"The first place you might look is Social Security," as USNews.com once said, regarding retirement funds. On the Social Security Administration's website, you can make a request for an official statement of your earnings record and estimated benefits, while verifying your legal retirement age (which varies depending on when you were born). The statement, ordered online, will arrive in the mail. To keep a clear picture of the benefits in your long-term plan, you should request a statement about every five years, checking it for unexpected changes or even errors. There are those people who believe that Social Security will disappear in a cloud of baby-boom dust any day now. That is improbable. For one thing, the slot-machine industry will never allow it to happen. However, those who would rather be safe than sorry should make financial plans on that basis; many people do, a trend that has increased the focus on personal retirement planning.

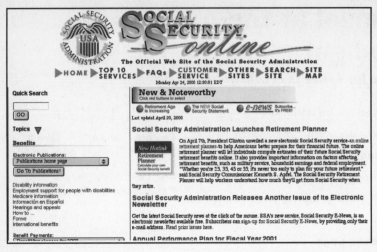

Even actuaries grow tired of numbers, sometimes. The result of break-time at the SSA is an amusing backwater on the site devoted to Name Distributions: the most popular first names, as found on Social Security applications, covering people born throughout the past 100 years. Rankings are sorted in any number of ways, but overall, most of the names have been Michael and Mary. The Name Distributions are shepherded by the Administration's chief actuary, whose first name is Michael. But perhaps you could have guessed that.

employee accounts

401Kafé.com
Corporate HQ: San Francisco, California

NO CHARGE

CALC.

ARCHIVE

The 401K is the tax-deferred retirement account maintained at work by employees of medium to large businesses. Beyond that statement, the 401K can be anything. If it were individual garden plots and not financial accounts that companies were supposed to provide, the image would not be so very different: a patchwork of plantings in a wide range of soils, as provided by companies. The 401Kafé offers a sensible, relaxed line of discourse about the accounts, appealing to both those people fascinated by them and those who are not. The FAQ section is the best place to start.

Often, Frequently Asked Questions are little more than bandages for poorly-edited websites—answering questions that should have been covered clearly elsewhere. At the 401Kafé, the FAQ section is more like a conversation, taking on a complex subject step-by-step. It is easy to read—and if you think that is a statement often made about detailed information on 401K plans, you are sadly mistaken.

The 401Kafé is a free offshoot of the 401K Forum, a site offering specific advice

for employees of contracted companies. The same group also maintains the IRA Junction, a site more rudimentary at this time than the 401Kafé.

The Vanguard site is full of mutual-fund news—that being one of Vanguard Group's favorite subjects—and it includes a very good edition of an online financial planner, too. The section of the site that shines, though, is the IRA section.

Vanguard.com
Vanguard Group
Corporate HQ: Valley Forge,
Pennsylvania

NO CHARGE   CALC.   ARCHIVE   E-COM

The IRA worksheet is a three-step process (with about 18 questions in all) that determines the preferable vehicle for your circumstances, the traditional IRA or the Roth version. (The difference between the two lies in the point at which taxes are to be paid on deposits.) Vanguard's worksheet is fully annotated, unlike many calculators, so that you not only get a final result, but understand exactly where it came from. The worksheet is truly worthwhile: My resulting totals on a $2,000 investment ranged at retirement age from about $8,500 in a Traditional to $10,150 in a Roth IRA. And in a regular, non-IRA account, the total would be about $5,700. If it is worth saving at all, it is worth understanding your options on an IRA account.

step three: tuition savings and scholarships
College is the price you have to pay for having smart kids

This step is the kindergarten of college—for you cannot go to classes until you learn to play. The jungle gym in question is the challenge of paying college tuition that seems treacherously steep from any angle. But to cite lighthearted analogies on such a subject may belie that fact that college tuition is too expensive and the means of relief (grants, loans, and scholarship) far too confusing. The fact that unassertive people pay more for college—or can't enroll—should be disturbing to us all. The sites in this step are for parents, guardians, and students who want to ensure that college is and remains financially viable, however absurd the game of it has become.

> ## Link List
> **AOA.dhhs.gov/retirement/
> default.htm**—retirement planning links
> **CollegeIsPossible.org/
> paying/paying_books.htm**—sources in all forms on college funding

well-rounded advice

Ed.gov/thinkcollege
U.S. Department of Education
HQ: Washington D.C.

NO CHARGE   SEARCH   CALC.   ARCHIVE

"Think College Early" is a special site established by the Department of Education to welcome neophytes into the process of preparing for college and applying for assistance. "Welcome" is the word of the day, and the homey graphics could be suited to a gift store. In a sense, of course, the Department of Education is a grand gift store, trying to give people the chance to go to college and sometimes paying them to do it. The site offers paths for three main forms of aid: Federal grants, Federal Student Aid (for which you can apply online), and HOPE scholarships. There is also a more general, step-by-step primer on obtaining Federal aid for college.

The site is called Think College Early, which is a good idea, of course. However, it could just as well be called Think College Late, because there is help throughout for adults returning for degrees at any age.

looking for help

FinAid.org
HQ: Pittsburgh, Pennsylvania

NO CHARGE   ARCHIVE

FinAid.org is a full service site dedicated to the procurement of college funding by loan, scholarship, or savings. That is a giant order to fill. A person of normal or lesser means ought to get a college degree just for figuring out how to pay for four years' tuition. FinAid.org offers more help than any other site, though it is heavily dependent upon links, and so it cannot be considered a one-stop answer to your questions. It features an array of 18 calculators, most of them pertaining to loan specifications, and often including tips for optimizing your situation, on paper and in reality. FinAid is at its best describing the types of loans available, and pointing to institutions offering each of them. It also explains alternative means of raising or saving money for tuition, such as trading national service for funding or taking advantage of prepaid tuition plans. These processes often require diligence well ahead of time. As to scholarship searches, it leaves that to six other sites, to which it is linked.

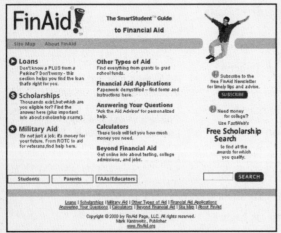

Forty one states now offer so-called Section 529 plans, based on a provision in the Federal tax code that grants special status to tuition savings accounts. States match that status, or offer some incentive, with programs intended to help middle-and low-income families accumulate more money faster. CollegeSavings.org is linked to each of the state-sponsored programs, so that you can familiarize yourself with the specifics of any program available to you. An even more aggressive approach is taken by SavingForCollege.com, a site operated by a pair of accountants in upstate New York. It contains state links, as well, but has a full bank of advice on making use of every bit of the potential of Section 529.

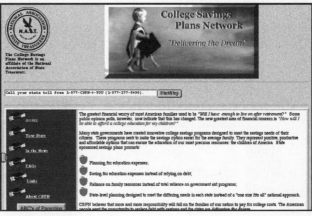

The College Board is the organization responsible for standardized testing, their best known product being the SAT, the Scholastic Aptitude Test. After the SAT has counseled you on college selection in two easy numbers (your scores) the College Board's website can follow up with further search tools. The Students and Parents section offers several searches, including those for colleges and even for careers. The most useful one financially, though, is the Scholarship search, involving an application about 20 questions long. Unlike some scholarship searches, including the aggressively mercenary FastWeb.com, the College Board runs a non-commercial site, on which privacy is assured. In a test I ran between it and FastWeb, CollegeBoard.org also offered by far the most scholarship opportunities.

just one more thing . . .

www.beeson.org/LivingTo100

HQ: Cambridge,
Massachusetts

NO CHARGE

CALC.

WELCOME TO

LIVING TO 100

LESSONS IN LIVING TO YOUR
MAXIMUM POTENTIAL AT ANY AGE

AND THE LIFE EXPECTANCY CALCULATOR©

This site is currently being hosted by the
Alliance for Aging Research.

You will be automatically taken to the
calculator, or you may click here to
be taken there now.

TOM SPEARS - AGE 102
CREDIT: MARIANNE HELM

ANNA MORGAN - AGE 101
CREDIT: ERIK SIMMONS

SISTERS WINIFRED WHYNOT (LEFT) - AGE 93
AND CATHERINE McCAIG (RIGHT) - AGE 102
CREDIT: BRIAN WALSKI, COURTESY OF THE
BOSTON HERALD

If being a millionaire isn't as rare as it once was, neither is living to the age of 100. The age inflation that has set in is a very welcome development, especially since so many centenarians are having as much fun as they ever did, with health and humor intact. Meanwhile, though, people are retiring much younger than ever before, meaning that savings and income need cover more than a few years: It must be enough for a half-a-lifetime. Perhaps you would like to know, for the sake of financial planning, just how long your golden years are going to extend. LivingTo100.com can make an educated guess. Dr. Thomas Perls of the Harvard Medical School undertook an important study of octogenarians in the mid-1990s and drew conclusions from it for a layman's book, *Living To 100*. The website of the same name offers his Life Expectancy Calculator, based on a series of two dozen questions about your personal habits. The results include the doctor's observations about those habits, and which ones can dramatically affect your lifespan. Dr. Perls' calculator told me that I would only make it to 92 years, which came as glad news, considering that a Gypsy fortune teller once predicted 86. The calculator made it clear that I could sail on a long way beyond 92 if only I gave up butter, and I'll think very seriously about doing that, over the next 50 or 60 years.

Planning and Saving

* The first rule is to start saving early in your career.

* If you failed to do that, then the second rule is to shrug off the first rule and start saving right now.

* Be guardedly pessimistic: Accept the fact that you are not going to win the lottery, inherit a fortune, or anything else between now and the day when you will require a plump savings account (be it for retirement or your child's college tuition).

* If your employer offers any sort of matching contribution plans, consider them carefully. In most cases, such plans are the closest you may ever come to finding free money.

* The time to investigate scholarships is when you are a freshman in high school. Identify the tuition grants for which you might qualify and then make sure that your high school record stands you in good stead for each. Sometimes this is a matter of receiving better grades, and there is nothing wrong with that, or volunteering for community service, and there is nothing wrong with that, either. In many cases, however, having a certain scholarship in your sights will simply encourage you to make notes on the activities or achievements that will bolster your scholarship application.

hopping on the internet:
the bizarre bazaar

The Internet can tell you where to shop, of course, but that is not the concern of this chapter, because much more importantly, it can tell you *how* to shop. You can be richer than you are, if only you know how to shop carefully.

Considering that the Internet is supposed to be the last word in technical sophistication, it has brought back a distinctly medieval atmosphere to shopping. Sellers stride into your domain like peddlers on donkeys, flashing deals and garish offers on banner ads. In this marketplace, there are crowds of shoppers and an array of worldly sellers, promoting methods of pricing that make getting a bargain on the Internet seem just as easy as choosing the walnut shell with the pea underneath it. Whether you are making purchases on the Net or merely gathering information to use at a local store, the only way to beat the pricing games is to walk all the way around the marketplace before plunking down a nickel. The Internet can help with that, too.

Spending money wisely is the part of finance that affects every household in America. No matter what the income, intelligent shopping makes a vast difference in the quality of life, as well as the amount of money left at the end of the day. It is a shame that frugality has such a bad reputation, as though it meant living on bread and water. The fact is that your best chance to live in a bit of luxury may just lie in the money you don't waste.

step one: investigation of products
Too much choice, the great Internet dilemma, is just as paralyzing as no choice at all

Just try and buy a good product when you don't know anything about it. Perhaps you've tried. Perhaps you have souvenirs of the experience cluttering up the closet. The sites in this step use various

Insiders' Tour of Yahoo!—Shopping:
(shopping.yahoo.com)

Yahoo! Shopping is the only place you need to go to find, compare and buy almost anything. With thousand of stores and million of products all in one place, you can shop by store, by brand, by product or by price.

Yahoo! Shopping offers a variety of features that significantly enhance the shopping experience. My Shopping is a personalized shopping page that allows for customization to fit your own shopping needs. You may view the status of recent orders, order history, your favorite stores, special offers and product suggestions. All of the information that's important to you may be organized any way you like. The Yahoo Shopping Gift Recommender suggest gifts based on the recipient, the price range, or the occasion. In addition, editor from high-profile publications offer gift suggestion in Editor's Picks.

To make the checkout process more convenient, Yahoo! shopping offers Yahoo! Wallet. Shop as many stores as you like, and checkout only once. Yahoo! Wallet securely stores your credit card, shipping and billing information. Simply choose Express Checkout and avoid the time-consuming task of filling in your personal information at each individual store.

Insiders' Tour of Yahoo!—Auctions
(auctions.yahoo.com)

Yahoo! Auctions allows users to buy and sell items online, auction style, with no commision fees for buyers or sellers. For sellers, Yahoo! has My Auction Booth, a personalized uniquely branded site for sellers to run their auctions. The sellers booth has a dedicated URL and allows sellers to customize the booth to meet their needs. In addition, Yahoo! offers sellers Auction Express, a tool that makes listing multiple items, even with pictures, a simple matter of a few clicks of a mouse.

Yahoo! Auctions also offers buyers and sellers Auction Alerts, so users will be told via email when their favorite sellers have listed a new item, or when a particular item they want has been put up to auction.

To make the process simple, Yahoo! Auctions provides a complete

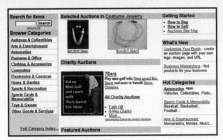

introduction for buyers or sellers new to online auctions, with a tour, a glossary, and thorough tutorials. The front page of Y! Auctions spotlights unique and appealing charity auctions.

methods to help you find the product in any major category that is best suited to you, in price, quality, and features.

best buys

www. ConsumersDigest.com

Consumer's Digest

Just because you can purchase anything in the world these days doesn't necessarily mean that you know what on earth you want. Sites such as ConsumersDigest.com help to narrow the field, sorting through items in the most popular shopping categories and offering an objective assessment.

ConsumersDigest.com is produced by the editors of *Consumer's Digest*. The site evaluates household goods from toasters to computers to cars. For each specific item, you will have a choice of more than 100 models, but the natural temptation is to take the shortcut straight to the site's Best Buys. The natural assumption is that all of the others are Dumb Buys—or, in other words, the sort of things with which your house is probably already filled. The Best Buys come in three designations, wherever appropriate: Premium, Mid-range, and Economy. The site's premium choice in vacuum cleaners, for example, is an Electrolux Guardian at $1,500. That is $300 more than I paid for my last car (though it did not come with a retractable cord). The choice in the mid-range was more like $200, and the economy cost about $100. Even aside from learning how the Bentley-set cleans their rugs, you can use ConsumerDigest.com as one of the better starting points for a shopping trip online.

product reviews

Productopia.com

Corporate HQ: San Francisco.
California

NO CHARGE   SEARCH   CALC.

Productopia conducts its own research on an even wider range of consumer products than those found at ConsumerDigest.com. The site rates household goods and electronics, but it also offers its opinion on toys, beauty items, and even fashion. There are 450 categories in all. Productopia will reveal only Top Picks (its own version of Best Buys); it doesn't bother with also-rans. There are nine such picks for each item: three each for quality, style, and value. Productopia insists very earnestly that its choices are not influenced by the fact that the company makes money linking interested customers to retailers. At any rate, it does not try to conceal the fact that such relationships are a fundamental part of its business. The site actively solicits customer experiences with products. Generally, they are of questionable value, except as an outlet for people disgruntled by real or imagined affronts. However, some comments are worth the eavesdropping, such as that of the woman who wrote of a certain vacuum cleaner: "They said on the radio it would pick up a bowling ball—it wouldn't even pick up a tennis ball!" Now you know: If your house is littered with unsightly bowling balls, don't count on vacuuming them up.

statistics and features

Personallogic.com

Division of America OnLine

HQ: San Diego, California

NO CHARGE   SEARCH   CALC.

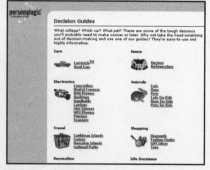

Personallogic.com has no opinions of its own, but offers copious data on a wide array of products. In a single category, for example, the one for digital cameras, the choice of models numbers 101. The information is presented in a simple chart, including capabilities, features, and warranties. If you are deciding between two or more models, you can easily customize a side-by-side comparison. The whole idea behind Personallogic is that you can make your own wise decisions, if you have the information at hand.

step two: investigation of prices

Whether or not you ultimately make your purchase online, you should have a very clear idea of the going price

When you want to locate the retailer with the best price on a specific model, these sites will do the looking for you.

PriceScan.com

NO CHARGE
SEARCH
CALC.

PriceScan is a universal aggregator, which is to say that it collects information on pricing from a wide variety of retailers, both those with e-commerce sites and those dealing strictly through the telephone and mail. In any case, PriceScan does not sell anything, but merely tells you how much a certain item will cost, across a field of 10 to 20 outlets. A certain Kodak digital camera could indeed be purchased for the manufacturer's suggested retail price of $799, according to PriceScan. That was at the bottom of a list of 18 retailers, though. At the top, the camera was available at $488. Another camera, an Agfa model, sold over a range from $79.99 to $129.00 (the list price). It is worth mentioning that some of the retailers with the lowest price on the Kodak were among the costliest for the Agfa. There is no single right answer among retailers, especially not on the Internet, and so dependence on an aggregator such as PriceScan can be vital.

Because the shipping cost can be a sneaky leveler where discount pricing is concerned, the PriceScan will, if you like, rank retailers according to the total cost (which includes shipping).

a profusion of product categories

Despite being headquartered in Israel, RUSure.com is an Americanized site, related largely to U.S. retail outlets. It provides price lists on a larger number of products and in a larger variety of categories than PriceScan, though the information is not sorted as neatly. You will have to read through fairly raw product price lists to confirm the model that you want and the price at which it is available. RUSure is

RUSure.com
Corporate HQ; Tel Aviv, Israel

NO CHARGE
SEARCH
CALC.

a cascade of product information, including extensive links to retail sites and others of interest to shoppers.

books and music

BestBookBuys.com
Corporate HQ: Altadena, California

NO CHARGE   SEARCH   QUOTES   E-COM

Personally, I think people should pay even more than the retail price for books (the extra could go directly to the author).

However, they seem to want to pay as little as possible instead, and to that end, BestBookBuys.com specializes in listing the cost of any title, as found all over the Internet. A price aggregator, BestBookBuys surveys more than 28 retail websites, including the colossus, Amazon.com, and an array of more obscure booksellers. The searching tool is downright dapper, it is so smooth in use, and you may be surprised at the range of prices, especially when shipping

is included as a factor. For those interested in browsing, the site has links to each of its represented sites, such as FatBrain.com (computer books) and CherryValleyBooks.com (children's books), which may open new worlds. For those strictly interested in buying one particular title, though, the site offers special discounts. Although you will make your purchase through the bookseller of your choice, it may prove a savings to you to get to it through BestBookBuys. The same company offers music through BestMusicBuys.com.

step three: strolling through the e-bazaar
The Internet offers a crop of new purchasing games

If you think that "retailing" refers to a shopkeeper putting a price on an item and then waiting for a customer, you have a lot of unlearning to do. First, forget that the shopkeeper sets the price; then forget that there is a set price, or that the shopkeeper has to wait for the customer. Then you can start to learn how to buy from the sites included in this step.

Volume purchasers receive a better pricing than a single unit. That is the fundamental fact behind wholesaling and the reason why you really should buy 45 televisions instead of one. You'd get a better unit price. MobShop.com tries to extend the same buying power to strangers by offering products with better and still better prices, depending on how many people contract to make a purchase during a certain time period (usually about a week). A certain flat-screen model, for example, was priced at $1,100, but would drop to $946 with the arrival of three more paying customers. Once they were onboard, the site would reveal the next challenge: the next price drop with the next incremental increase in buyers. You won't know how low the price will go until the buying period is over.

Keep in mind that the selection of products is not extensive on MobShop or, indeed, on most of the following retail sites. They are not full-range stores, so you might not find your first choice among brands and models.

group buying

MobShop.com

Corporate HQ: San Francisco, California

NO CHARGE   SEARCH   QUOTES   E-COM

HaggleZone is really something of a game. First you choose a product: that is standard for a shopping expedition. Next, however, you choose your adversary from a group of six hagglers; they have names and personalities, and are represented by photographs, but the process is programmed. In other words, it may be real-time, but that doesn't make it spontaneous. While dickering over a Kodak camera, for example, that lists at $799, a haggler named a price of $736. I typed in my bid of $400, and she responded in writing with a pithy comment and a counter offer of $701. I typed in my next offer and received more cajoling and a slightly lower price in response. You are invited to haggle without any obligation and make your purchase only if you are satisfied with the resulting price. I didn't find particularly low prices, but then maybe I am not the greatest of hagglers. One thing that did disturb me, however, is that I received different final prices each time I tried for my Kodak camera.

give and take

HaggleZone.com
Netmarket Group

HQ: Stamford, Connecticut

NO CHARGE   SEARCH   QUOTES   E-COM

inviting bids

LiquidPrice.com

Information Management Associates

Corporate HQ: Redwood, California

NO CHARGE   SEARCH   QUOTES   E-COM

LiquidPrice is a lazy man's sort of a store: The customer picks out a product, and then retailers come through with their best prices. The site, which requires free registration for use, offers products in a fairly wide range of electronics and household products. It is quite a simple matter to pick out a product and then invite retailers to send you their best shot at a closing deal. They do so by leaving e-mails in your registered account on the site.

profiting from others' mistakes

Overstock.com

Corporate HQ: Salt Lake City, Utah

NO CHARGE   SEARCH   QUOTES   E-COM

If you are flexible in what you want, then Overstock.com can offer some of the lowest of all prices on the Internet. The selection is not great at any one time—about 800 items in many categories from appliances to watches—because the nature of the business is in over-stocks. Overstocks are boo-boos, so they are a bit unpredictable. However, a Swiss watch, with a range of $70 to $140 on PriceScan, cost only $55 at Overstock.com. On the other hand, a Panasonic VCR, with a range of $274 to $498 on PriceScan, cost $349 at Overstock. Such liquidation sites aren't normally covered by aggregators such as PriceScan, because the items do not remain in stock for more than a few days or weeks.

step four: don't get carried away

Auctions are as much fun online as they are in person . . . for the auctioneer

The beauty of online auctions is that they bring individuals together in retailing. Businesses are part of the melee, too, but the power and excitement of sites such as Ebay stem from the fact that anyone with something to sell now has a customer base of 10 million or more. That is slightly more than those who ramble up to the average garage sale.

In the olden days of a few years ago, people would walk around antiques shows wearing T-shirts trumpeting whatever item the wearer was interested in buying: "Collector Seeks 1940s Dish-drainers," for example. There was nothing so obscure that someone somewhere didn't have one—or want one. The frustration was knowing that whatever it was you wanted was out there, somewhere, but where? I used to imagine myself skywriting the names of the vintage books I wanted: rather low-tech, but I was on the right track. The single triumph of the Internet may be the use of a trillion dollars worth of computers to match every possible collector with every known collectible. Ebay.com is the hub of the new collecting frenzy, thanks largely to its long list of items, along with a powerful search engine by which to find anything fast. However, this section on shopping is not so much about indulging in a fetish for dish-drainers, but rather about saving money on items even more essential—if such a thing is possible.

Ebay may have started out as an auction dedicated to antiques, but it carries new items, too, sold by jobbers or even retailers. The pleasant surprise is that practically every product, in every model and shade, is available on Ebay. The dismaying surprise, however, is that Ebay bidding takes on a life of its own, and some new items go for more money on Ebay than they fetch at regular retail websites. (Does that give you an idea for a money-making scheme?) The key, as a bidder, is to go through the steps above and know your pricing before you get caught up in the bidding on any auction site.

Ebay may be the name you know, but there are other auction sites on the Internet. BiddersEdge.com offers a means to search about 80 of them (including Ebay, in a separate stroke) all at once. According to the site, it sifts through a total 5.2 million items, at a single stroke. I haven't checked that number myself. However, I did once see an item on Ebay that did not bob up in the exact search on BiddersEdge. So, let's say it sifts more like 5.1 million items, just to be on the safe side. The site has links to all 80 of the auctions it represents.

person to person

Ebay.com
Corporate HQ: San Jose, California

NO CHARGE   SEARCH   QUOTES   E-COM

multi-auction search

BiddersEdge.com
Corporate HQ: Burlington, Massachusetts

NO CHARGE   SEARCH

BiddersEdge gives a little more added value in the form of the Inside Edge, weekly columns that follow developments and noteworthy items in many different auction categories. Each column even includes a chart, akin to a stock-price chart, that tracks the pricing trend of a specific collectible or product.

business to person

UBid.com
Corporate HQ: Chicago, Illinois

NO CHARGE   QUOTES   E-COM

In the field of business-to-person auctions (as opposed to person-to-person auctions, such as Ebay), retailers put new products on the block. At UBid.com, you will be dealing with a company, which may make you feel more comfortable, especially when buying new items. UBid has an extensive number of product categories, from clothing and electronics to autographs and off-lease (reconditioned) computers.

just one more thing . . .

ShoppingList.com
Corporate HQ: Sunnyvale, California

NO CHARGE   SEARCH

ShoppingList.com is a conduit between the Internet and the real world, offering specifics on sale-priced products at the stores in your own local area. You can search nearby sales either by product, seeing all the televisions on sale, or by store, calling up what amounts to a paperless store flyer. The sale listings are largely drawn from national chains, though another section of ShoppingList is as local as the Chinese restaurant, dry cleaners, or sandwich shop down the street.

Saving money on purchases is an obligation in a well-run household, whatever the income, but for some shoppers, it is a professional sport. They will especially like the "Ask Jeannette" column on the site: She is something of a coach, reminding you, for example, that the best time to buy a car at a dealership is late on the last day of the month.

> ### Short Shots
>
> **ActiveBuyersGuide.com**— comprehensive product education and comparison (see also chapter XII, Online Brokerages).
>   —IShip.com-calculates cost of shipping by various concerns
>   —WeeklyFreebie.com-giveaways

Auction Action
Part One: Power Buyers
Tips for Online Bidding

The two largest auction sites, Yahoo! Auctions and Ebay, list more than 500,000 fresh items every day, augmenting the millions already there. Typically, a little more than half of the items are second-hand—antiques and collectibles. The remainder consists of new merchandise and services.

Learning by Browsing:
Just now, I looked up the great racehorse Secretariat on Ebay, and found items including the Virginia farm on which he was born, complete with its own one-mile racetrack: $5.9 million.

1. NEW MERCHANDISE . . . Whenever you are bidding on new merchandise, know the retail price in the real world. Too many bidders get caught up in the auction, and pay more for an item than it would cost at Sears, or any other regular retailer. Services such as those listed in Step Two can help, or you can call around to stores in your area. A rule of thumb is to bid no more than two-thirds of what the item would cost at a retail establishment, online or off not one penny more.

Learning by Browsing:
Just now, an online-auction listing for new Kodak DC280 cameras recorded the four most recent winning bids (found under Completed Sales) as $446, $475, $492, and $495. *But look:* At this moment, PriceScan.com lists 28 retailers who are selling the DC280 for less than $495— and six who are selling it at less than $446. That being the case, a bid of about $310 would be plenty, considering the extra risk in dealing with an unknown seller, as opposed to an established retailer.

2. COLLECTIBLES . . . For collectors, the prime attraction of Internet auctions is the selection of it. It may as well be limitless. I thought I was the only person in the world with a weakness for the old-time actor George Arliss, but the first time I tried out an online auction and pessimistically checked his name, the listing showed fifteen or twenty items of Arliss-abilia. It was an affecting moment, to learn that I was no longer alone in this Arliss universe—and make no mistake, that feeling of shared identity is a driving factor in the success of online auctions. Many people bid to cry out who they are. That may sound rather dramatic, but beware of

3. SHARPS . . . Because of the emotion, excitement, and increasingly large sums passing through online auctions, con-artists have moved in. Here is one thing that they know: No one expects to find a bargain in plain sight. The bargains are only to be found where the buyer does not quite know what he or she has.

Learning by Browsing:

A few months ago, I wanted a certain book about a 1908 car race and looked anxiously under "1908 race," where all such items tended to be and where most of the sites fetched frenzied prices. However, when I searched under the author's name one day, I happened to hit on the book, which was being sold by someone who thought it was about an airplane pilot. I was the only bidder, and it was something of a bargain—only because it wasn't offered under "1908 race."

As the Sharps, they want to create an impression of ignorance. They want you to think that you know more than they do. And so it is that items are vaguely described, with just enough clues to lead you to an erroneous conclusion. In 1999, the description of an abstract painting was peppered with just enough tips to make dozens of people conclude that it must be the work of a famous painter named Clyfford Still (a relatively famous painter, anyway.) After 73 bids, a computer professional in Virginia paid $30,000 for it, borrowing the money against his retirement account. It turned out to be worthless. A year later, he told the *San Francisco Chronicle* that it was "sitting in the closet. It will sit there until I pay it off—at which time, I may destroy it."

Don't bid a lot for anything that 1) you haven't seen in person; 2) isn't positively identified, or 3) can't be returned if it isn't satisfactory. You have to define "a lot," as a minimum expenditure, for yourself. Don't think in terms of how much you can afford to lose on a bad transaction, though: Try to think of how much a conartist would need as a minimum to bother with a scam.

3. SHILLS . . . It costs a quarter to list an item on Ebay, nothing at all to list one on Yahoo! Auctions. If Seller Sandy decides to bid on his or her own item in order to boost the price, then the total liability, should no other bidders come along, is somewhere between nothing and 25 cents. In a few weeks, Sandy can just put the item back on and start over. Shilling is ever so tempting in online auctions, and a great many sellers do it. There aren't too many ways you are going to ferret them out while you are bidding, but here are three points to remember. First, examine the item to your heart's content and then take out a piece of paper and write down

the price you are willing to pay. Place the piece of paper near your computer screen. Simple as it is, that is one of the best ways to keep from getting caught up and over bidding.

Second, enter separate bids until the auction winds down to its last couple of hours. The online auctions offer what Ebay calls "proxy" bidding, by which you can enter your highest bid and the computerized "auctioneer" will bid incrementally for you, whenever you are outbid by someone else. Needless to say, that someone else could be the seller. With days to spare, Seller Sandy will place bids under other names, exploring the limits of your proxy bid, nudging it up bit by bit. Sandy knows that even if he or she finally tops your proxy bid, you will probably be back over the course of the remaining days, to place *one last* bid. Because the action heats up so fiercely in the last 15 seconds of some auctions, though, you probably want to enter your top bid as a proxy with a few minutes or hours to spare.

Third, the seller who lists an item with a "reserve" (a secret minimum below which the item will not sell) is at least acknowledging that he or she will not shill the bidding to ensure a profit. The reserve will do that, though it costs the seller several dollars. A seller with a reserve may shill out of sheer and wanton greed, but nonetheless, the presence of a reserve (duly noted with the item description) is some indication of a dispassionate seller.

Auction Action
Part Two: Empowered sellers
Tips for Online Auction

1. Stay in close communication with the winning bidder, keeping him or her abreast of each stage of the transactions: that, for example, the payment has been received, the item has been packed, and finally, that it has been shipped. Short, chipper e-mails such as these generate positive comments.

2. Detailed descriptions, even when a picture is included, appear to spark more bidding. Walk the prospective buyer around the item, pointing out even things that can be seen in the picture.

3. Spell everything correctly in the tag. People looking for a model of a Ford Fairlane will not be searching for "Farelane" or "Fairlain."

4. Think long and hard about the descriptive tag, getting in as many different terms as possible. As a rule of thumb, make sure that your item will show up on three different searches, ones that are heavily trafficked. Test individual words or pairs of words from your tag. It is easy

to test in advance. Let's say, for example, that we are selling an original copy of the Declaration of Independence. This is a bad tag:

"Declaration of Independence—Original Copy"

In refining a better tag, you'll find that no one really searches for adjectives. Shorten the phrase, "Original Copy," in an intriguing way. Another trick in shortening tags: Don't use punctuation *and* a space between words. One or the other will do.

Second, put some other names in there. Searching for items pertinent to each of the prominent signers, you'll find that Thomas Jefferson receives the most attention. Testing further, you'll see that "Jefferson," all by itself, is too broad.

A third direction from which to attract searches is through the historical time frame. Dates, such as "1770s," are ineffective, though. Use the popular name for the era. "Revolutionary" comes up with items that are heavily bid.

Here is a good tag, because it can attract bidders using three different search terms: Declaration of Independence REAL!—Thomas Jefferson—Revolutionary

Surely, someone would buy it.

Shopping on the Internet

The Long and Short of

* Know the following three things before buying anything online: 1) the address of the company with which you are dealing; 2) the return policy as it relates specifically to the item you are buying; 3) the final *total* amount that will be charged to your credit card.

* When you are comparing prices, make sure that you are seeing prices for precisely the same exact model. Write down the numbers, weights, number of pixels, etc.

* Shipping costs make a difference in the final price, as you must be aware. Some companies only charge you the exact door-to-door charges, and that is the fairest way, since UPS and heavier U. S. Postal Service packages vary according to distances.

T ravel:
the world wide hub

You *can* find better fares or better itineraries: it has become a fact, and a very welcome one. Flexibility has always been the first factor in getting either, but with the chance to see all of your options on the Internet, that does not necessarily require a sacrifice.

As the travel industry evolved in the twentieth century, it became something of a blind maze, especially for cost-conscious customers. In speaking to a booking agent, you had to ask just the right questions in order to find out the cheapest way to go somewhere. In most cases, you couldn't simply say: what is the cheapest itinerary? You could only ask in your formal deposition if it would make a difference if you left Tuesday, and what about Wednesday—and what I flew through Pittsburgh? The Internet has opened the gates of information for budget travelers and any others who simply want to make their plans based on *all* available information.

step one: booking a trip
Bypass the travel agency and plan your own itinerary

The sites in Step One take you from here to there as quickly as possible—"here" meaning the moment when you realize that you want to be someplace else for awhile and "there" meaning the moment when you have a trip all planned. Trip.com is a full-service site, the best of that burgeoning field, while the other sites listed have specialized approaches to the business of booking your travels.

LastMinuteTravel.com does not expect you to leave town by sunset, or anything that hectic. Many of the deals offered stretched out as far as sixty days in advance. The site describes itself as a fulfillment service, which means that it does not actually book travel, but merely lists

travels fastest

LastMinuteTravel.com

Corporate HQ: Atlanta, Georgia

NO CHARGE   SEARCH   QUOTES   E-COM

special offers tendered by hotels, airlines, and other travel companies hoping to find customers for otherwise unsold space. The airline listings are the strongest feature of the site, as choices abound for most itineraries: Coach, business-class, and first-class tickets are all likely to be offered. Some tickets have specific dates attached, while others can be booked for convenience over a longer span. Some people naturally use the site's searching tool by choosing a departure city and a destination, while others select certain dates and then look at what is avail-

Insiders' Tour of Yahoo!—Travel
(travel.yahoo.com)

The reservations service at Yahoo! Travel can book airline flights, car rentals, hotel accommodations, cruises and vacation packages. Even without registering, you can check schedules and prices for trips still in the planning stage. The Best Fare Finder will instantly inform you of the least expensive flights between two airports on certain days. It is especially useful if you are not particular about your travel times or routes. Under My Trips, found on the homepage, you can check the flight time of any current or imminent flight, whether the flight was booked through Yahoo! Travel or not.

TIP: The Specials section of Yahoo! Travel's reservation service highlights little known travel bargains, such as cottages in resort areas, in addition to last minute sales in every travel category.

If you are browsing for travel ideas, Yahoo! Travel offers suggestions sorted by Destination (i.e. Asia), Activity (i.e. ,golf), and Lifestyle (i.e., families with children). The site's lively Travel Community is another source for tips to make your

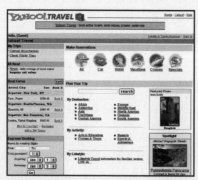

travels the best they can be. It consists of hundreds of clubs devoted to a specific destination or activity, with members trading experiences and advice. Yahoo! Travel also offers current and archived news stories pertaining to travel bargains.

NO CHARGE   SEARCH   E-COM

able for them. Alternatively, you can specify a certain travel brand. I always thought myself a peculiar sort of vacationer, in that I hardly care at all where a plane is going, so long as it is Lufthansa Airlines. LastMinuteTravel.com easily accommodates loyalists such as me. On the Lufthansa list, for one example, was a roundtrip ticket from New York or Boston to anywhere in Europe for $255. If I had one of those in my pocket, this would be my last minute in New York.

SkyAuction is an especially natty site, which is not surprising considering its home address is on Madison Avenue in New York City. As an auction, it is also comprised of items intriguing enough to stir up considerable froth in the bidding. Amid the many airline tickets on the block was the opportunity to go all the way around the world, courtesy of a twelve-airline consortium, on an itinerary of your own devising. The bidding was at $2,001 with one day to go. Hotel rooms, cruises, and package vacations are also on the SkyAuction block. The site bills itself at the top of its homepage as "The No Reserve Travel Auction," implying that if no one else bids, you can grab something with a bid as low as $1. But that is wishful thinking: The complete Terms and Conditions, which are somewhat less prominently displayed, refer specifically to the fact that the site does have reserve bids, and only those offers meeting or exceeding them will actually be sold.

online auction

SkyAuction.com
Corporate HQ: New York City, New York

Of all of the travel agency sites, Trip.com evinces the most enthusiasm for travel, both for the endless adventure of moving about the planet and for the steeplechase of finding the best itinerary at the best price. As at other full-service sites, you can be your own travel agent, looking for flights, rates, rooms, rental cars, and so forth. TheTrip.com goes far beyond that, though, offering tools that actually serve to coach you in the sport mentioned above: that steeple-

super agents

Trip.com
Coportate HQ: Englewood, Colorado

chase of booking a good trip, cheap. FareAware allows you to choose two cities and see the recent history of fares between them, so that you can get an idea of just exactly what a fair price might be. FareAware not only supplies an industry average, for a particular season in the year, but also informs you of the airline with the lowest fares on average. Trip.com also has airport maps, a world clock, a link to travel news, and, most fascinating of all, the Flightracker. For any flight that is actually inflight, the Flightracker will note its exact location, its speed, altitude, and so forth. Even after you book a trip on Trip.com, company travel agents will examine the details and, if possible, suggest ways to reduce the cost.

Other online travel agencies tend to be much less effusive: They are best regarded as booking agents and are competent at that. Expedia.com (Bellevue, Washington) is a clean-looking site; one of its helpful features will suggest hotels in the vicinity of any address you submit. Travel.AmericanExpress.com (New York City, New York) will allow you to look at schedules and rates without formally registering. Travelocity.com (Ft. Worth, Texas) is the largest of the online travel agents. Closely associated with the Sabre reservations system, it can book a seat on 95% of the airline flights around the world. Travelocity, which merged with PreviewTravel, also represents 40,000 hotels and 50 car rental companies.

a room for the night

Quikbook.com
Corportate HQ: New York City, New York

NO CHARGE   SEARCH   QUOTES   E-COM

Quikbook.com's expertise is the hotel world, and it does not deviate from its speciality. Overall, the rates that it finds are a shade better than those at other sites, including full-service travel agencies such as those listed above. The most impressive aspect of Quikbook.com, though, is the amount of information it offers on each of the properties it represents. Descriptions of each property stretch for three or four screens, covering amenities, directions, specifications, advisories, and even comments solicited by Quikbook from clients. Quite a number of hotel-reservations sites seem to consider hotels—and probably customers—to be bland items, merely to be matched and dispatched. Quikbook.com, however, does not merely toss you into any hotel, a difference that will give you cause to appreciate it at some point on your trip.

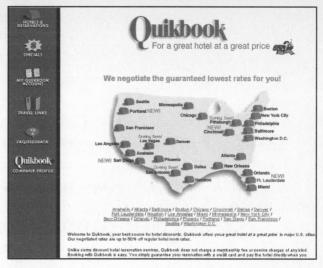

Reservation information and even rates are likely to be at their best on individual company sites, especially for air travel and car rental. Thrifty's notably well-designed site illustrates one good example. Its searching tool, the main feature of the site, is very easy to use—you can tell it everything it needs to know just by clicking away (for those of us who are sometimes too lazy to expend energy by typing). But when bookings are otherwise hard to come by, the site can suggest variances in car size or locale that may effect a match. I had that experience on an occasion of unique frustration, when I couldn't get a car in Detroit, of all places. The Thrifty site, using its ability to look a little to the left and right where most travel sites can only stare blankly ahead, found a way. Whenever the larger sites fail you, brand name sites such as Thrifty.com should be used as a second line of attack.

car rental

Thrifty.com

Corporate HQ; Tulsa, Oklahoma

NO CHARGE · QUOTES · E-COM

airline phenomenon

FlyAOW.com

Airlines of the Web

HQ: Menlo Park, California

NO CHARGE · QUOTES · ARCHIVE · E-COM

FlyAOW.com is the hub of all hubs for airlines, or at least for their websites. As noted above, it is a very good idea to contact airline sites directly, especially if you are otherwise unable to make your bookings just the way you want them. FlyAOW.com can direct you to individual sites or to at least telephone lines for every airline in operation around the world. That is an eminently practical feature, but what if you want a site for an airline that is not in operation? FlyAOW, rife with airlines, even gives a choice in non-airlines: First, there is a long list of links to virtual airlines, cyber playthings which never were . . . but are. Second, there are links to sites dedicated to defunct airlines, such as Braniff or Laker, which once were . . . but now are not. Getting back to the practical aspects of FlyAOW.com, there is a CyberFare service, which will locate fares and other travel rates for you and connect you to sellers. The site will also alert you when a desired itinerary drops to a specified price.

FlyAOW.com also provides links to government weather agencies in practically every nation around the world.

step two: money savers and adventure
Just be flexible and the world will be at your feet

You know that traveling has become a drag when: 1) you care whether the hotels you book have HBO; 2) you might even like having Sbarro pizza for breakfast; 3) you no longer buy postcard stamps before you depart, and 4) you don't even reset your watch when the plane is landing. The following sites will help return anyone to the advanture that traveling should be.

— Link List —

Mercurio.iet.unipi.it/misc/ links/html—Worldwide railroads
TravelZoo.com—discount travel sites

traveling light

CourierTravel.org
Global Courier
HQ: Nederland, Colorado

NO CHARGE   SEARCH   QUOTES

Materials accompanied by a person clear customs checkpoints more quickly than those shipped as cargo. For that reason, legitimate companies seeking to offer the fastest possible delivery of international shipments provide drastically reduced airline fares to travelers willing to forego checked baggage. Several travel associations match willing passengers to tickets, charging an annual membership fee for the service. CourierTravel.org charges $40 for such a membership, but it has one of the few sites that will allow you to browse the fares currently available before joining. Those fares, which can even drop down to nothing on some routes, are indeed rather tempting: roundtrip New York-to-Tokyo for $300, for example, or New York-to-Beijing (roundtrip) for $250. Flying to Beijing, China, as a courier, with only a toothbrush (or whatever else fits in your carry-on) is the stuff of Warner Brothers movies. The man seated next to you on the plane is obviously going to be Sidney Greenstreet. Courier-

Travel.org offers complete details of the courier process and even evaluates its major competitors; it likes some and dislikes others, but it encourages you to visit all of them through links.

If leaving one home empty so that you can go and pay good money to rent another home in the form of a hotel seems rather inefficient to you, then you will like the self-evident idea behind HomeExchange.com. Individuals use the site to describe their homes, a service that costs $30 per year. The rest of us can search the site without charge and then contact the owners of any likely property, hoping to entice them into a swap. Most of the properties being offered are upper middle-class homes: an ocean front cottage on Martha's Vineyard or a condominium in Boston, for example. The locations alone can suggest a vacation, as with a farmhouse in County Donegal, Ireland or an ocean front villa being offered in Benen, on the west coast of Africa. It comes complete with a couple of four-wheel drive cars and servants, too. The Donegal farmhouse has a cat you have to feed. To me, the hard part is not picking out a place to stay, but in figuring out how to pass my own house off as a vacation spot. If I could do that, I'd be in Africa right now, asking the servants to push my chaise a little closer to the ocean. Not too close.

trading places

HomeExchange.com

Corporate HQ: Santa Barbara, California

NO CHARGE   SEARCH

The sad fact is that the word, "freighter," is turn-off. It sounds like ropes—on the deck, in the food, under the mattress. However, "low-key cruising" would be a better description of freighter travel.

Conventional cruising has the unfortunate characteristic of bringing along onboard everything one is taking to sea to leave behind. I refer to discotheques and loud music, of course; to schedules and to places to be, and most of all, to strangers in large numbers. How could any of that be relaxing? This low-key cruising offers

officers quarters

FreighterWorld.com

Freighter World Cruises

Corporate HQ: Pasadena, California

NO CHARGE   SEARCH   QUOTES

Short Shots

BNM.com—all about rental cars

Travel.stat.gov/passport_ services.html—and don't wait 'til the last second

accommodations on par with most cruiseships, but in far smaller numbers. Most freighters have room for 6 to 12 passengers. FreighterWorld.com places 1,200 clients each year on freighter cruises lasting two weeks to 120 days. A round-the-world voyage on an English or German ship costs about $7,000 per person. Cunard, at Cunardline.com, is the last passenger line to offer Transatlantic passage, but FreighterWorld lists several freight companies that also offer Atlantic service: One especially well-fitted ship sails from Savannah, Georgia, to Valencia, Spain, a balmy sounding course.

just one more thing . . .

Oanda.com
Olsen & Associates

Corporate HQ: Zurich, Switzerland and New York City, New York

NO CHARGE

CALC.

With an array of tools for analyzing the profitability of currency exchange, Oanda.com could be listed in an investment section of this book. However, it also caters gladly to travelers of the sort who wander around the world befuddled as to whether they are supposed to multiply their Albanian Leks by .06 or multiply their U.S. dollars by minus 2, in order to find out how much anything costs. For such travelers, Oanda.com offers a Quick Converter, a chart pitting any two of 164 world currencies against each other. It is neatly presented on one page, ready to be printed out and leaned upon heavily on market day in the village square. A more complex chart can also be requested showing the exchange rates of any six currencies against each other. Oanda doesn't merely convert monies; it is just as facile with languages, as the pages can be read in any of seven languages, at the click of button.

Travel

The Long and Short of

* Even after making reservations through a general service travel site, check the same plans with the respective airline, hotel or car rental company. If you find higher prices quoted, then hurry back to your reservations. However, you may be surprised to find lower ones quoted.

* If you must make a trip without advance notice, airline tickets can be prohibitively expensive. In that case, be especially open-minded about times or routes—more and more, airlines are starting to offer eleventh-hour sales on selected flights.

* For purchases in foreign countries, credit cards usually extend a more advantageous exchange rate than local banks and other currency changers.

Taxes and law:
rules of order

Two of the most serious obligations related to your overall finances are income taxes and legal matters. Taxes are somewhat predictable. Legal matters, on the other hand, are bound to arise, yet it is hard to plan for them in advance. Both demand your keenest attention, though. You must keep both in mind when you begin to build your finances.

A good citizen understands the government's dual obligations to collect taxes and to uphold laws, and respects those prerogatives. Enjoying either process is another matter, however. In this chapter, we attempt the nearly impossible: making tax filing a breeze, a veritable jamboree. Maybe when the government realizes that everyone in the country is having a wonderful time filling out tax forms, perhaps it will even come to its senses and outlaw them.

In legal dealings, the crucial step is finding an excellent, disciplined, and honorable lawyer. Struggling along with the wrong lawyer is a bad proposition, though people often feel constrained to do just that, for the lack of a choice. To that end, we have included sites that offer lawyer-searching tools, and some grounding in legal matters so that you can effectively interview candidate attorneys. The quality of your choice will make a significant difference.

step one: help yourself to lower taxes
Deducting the stress from income-tax filing is a long-term project

If you hire a service to prepare your tax form, it only means that you are off the hook for one day per year; April 15th, of course. Nonetheless, the taxes are still yours to pay—and so are the finances that underlie them. The sites below will give you information for those other 364 days, when you are making the decisions that make an impact on your taxes. These sites are even more helpful for those who, in the lonely gloom of April 14th's last few hours, fill out the forms for

Insiders' Tour of Yahoo!—Taxes and Law
(taxes.yahoo.com)

Even before starting to fill out the first form, visitors can improve their efficiency by looking at the Tax Preparation Checklist, which points out the materials you should have on hand, from proof of assets to personal data. The Tax Center has a long list of tips for the taxpayer, covering subjects from educational expenses to employment. There is also pages of advice aimed at investors, provided by Fairmark.com.

TIP: Yahoo! Finance's Tax Center offers links to other important tax sites, including the Internal Revenue Service site.

At tax time, you can file your return electronically at Yahoo! Finance's Tax Center for $9.95. The section also provides advice and tips for taxpayers. Among the tools offered at the Tax Center is a tax estimator, which can help predict the refund to which you are entitled. In addition, there is a tax calculator, a calendar, and a complete glossary of tax terms.

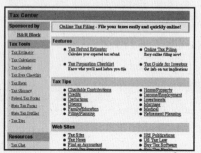

TIP: Yahoo! Finance offers all current federal and state income tax forms, which can be downloaded for your use.

NO CHARGE   CALC.

By the time you are filling out your income tax forms, it is already too late to take advantage of the very best tax tips. Streamlining that crunch time is the impetus behind Deloitte & Touche's Tax Planning Guide, an eight-chapter course that describes long-term planning techniques such as income shifting and investment evaluation. It also includes a chart that leaves little doubt about the advantages of tax-deferred investment. Intelligent and unrushed, this is the sort of thinking that should be honed over years—not patched together in the nick of time on December 31st or April 14th. Just a bit more urgent is D&T's tax calendar, which lays out the financial priorities quarter by quarter throughout the coming year. The site also has a page detailing tax-law changes instituted since the preceding year. For those looking for some magic bullet at filing time, D&T has a long list of tax tips, sorted according to the type of people who might benefit most from them: there are seven tips for executives, for example, and 21 for people with high incomes. Even when the rich don't get richer, on this site they can keep from getting poorer.

DTOnline.com
Deloitte & Touche
Corporate HQ: Cincinnati, Ohio

NO CHARGE   CALC.

Bearing down on the actual 1040, Jackson Hewitt's website offers tax information in a format well suited to the Web. There are 19 general subjects, and taxtips in 13 categories such as medical expenses and real estate. Some of the general information is delivered in Question-and-Answer form, which is easy to skim, if difficult to absorb as a cohesive body. The heading of one section is in question form: "Am I an employee or self-employed?" Having tried to manage a worker or two who never could answer that question, I thought Jackson Hewitt's answer kept to the tax ramifications of consultancy (and not the loyalty of lone wolves). Another aspect of JacksonHewitt.com that is worth perusing at tax time is its list of the Top Fifty Overlooked Deductions.

JacksonHewitt.com
Jackson Hewitt
Corporate HQ: Parsippany, New Jersey

NO CHARGE   CALC.   ARCHIVE   E-COM

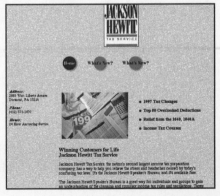

more tips

TaxHawk.com
Scott Rasmussen, CPA
Corporate HQ: Phoenix,
Arizona

NO CHARGE

TaxHawk is a quiet, peaceable site, despite its predatory name. It has nothing to sell, no causes to pound or expound. Even more remarkable, the page describing the originator of the site contains but three short lines: all in all, very low key. In place of hype, TaxHawk offers a thorough Tax Deduction Dictionary, one that elaborate on the nuances of the trickier deductions, such as hobby losses. The site also has specific advice on 14 topics in unique but very useful categories such as Your Parents, Your Children, and Your Job. The section on audit prevention is well worth reading since the bother of an audit is often initiated by small discrepancies of the sort highlighted by TaxHawk. The site's Top Ten Tax Tips are also insightful—not mundane at all, as tips of all types too often are.

government tax center

IRS.gov
Department of the Treasury,
Internal Revenue Service
HQ: Washington D.C.

NO CHARGE   ARCHIVE

The IRS is probably depicted in the back of your mind as a shady figure in a Fedora hat, but that same IRS surprised everyone recently by producing a downright colorful site for the Internet. Called the "Digital Daily," the site boasts quite a catchy name coming from a group whose previous best effort at a title was something like, "4562, Depreciation and Amortization." The Digital Daily divides its tax information into two parts: for individuals and for businesses. While we've all heard of how inaccurate IRS advice can be, rendered in person or over the phone, the topics on the website, however, are thorough discussions, and presumably accurate. Any new advice or interpretation that you receive from another website or any other source ought to be checked against the related topic at IRS.gov. If you want an even deeper understanding of tax law, the site includes what it calls, merrily enough, "Regulations in English." It recounts the complete tax code in language simplified from the legal version. Of course, the reason that original code was written in "legalese," is that it must withstand the fracturing effects of interpretation; the more exacting the language, the narrower the scope of interpretation. Gray areas exist, nonetheless, and that brings us back to Taxpayer Assistance. You may have to ask the IRS a question. It can't be done online, as of this writing, but the IRS website includes a list of offices and toll-free numbers around the country.

The IRS's website is also a source for all tax publications, including forms, which can be downloaded and printed at your home or office.

advice on retainer

TaxHotLine.net
TaxRite
Corporate HQ: Arlington, Illinois

For $49.95 per year, TaxRite will place a team of enrolled agents, CPAs, tax lawyers, and former auditors at your disposal, to answer as many tax-related questions as you care to submit. While you can't ask the questions online, only on the telephone, you can learn more about the service through the website, TaxHotLine.net. The staff is not available to fill out your current forms, but they will look over your previous filings and make suggestions.

filing online

Wwwebtax.com
Corporate HQ: Houston, Texas

Jackson Hewitt reports that 95 percent of its customers opt to file their federal income taxes online. According to the IRS, one in six taxpayers does so, and a gaggle of sites has emerged to assist taxpayers in filing online. Wwwebtax.com has considerable experience in the field, considering how new the field actually is, in that it is a subsidiary of WorldWideWeb Tax, a company that produces tax-preparation software for professionals. The site also maintains an extensive tax encyclopedia, easily searched by term. Though no direct assistance is available for filling out forms, you can file electronically through Wwwebtax.com at a cost of $9.95.

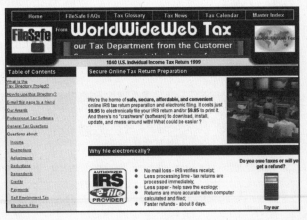

Another site, TaxCut.com, also offers online filing at a cost of $9.95. For e-filers, refunds are typically returned within eight days; for anyone who needs the money sooner than that, TaxCut.com offers loans against expected refunds of up to $5,000. That practice, a common one at tax services, is usually over priced as a form of borrowing.

Fidelity.com has been known to offer free e-filing, using the Quicken TurboTax package, but whether that largess will continue every year is uncertain. HDVest.com (Irving, Texas) has also offered free preparation and filing in the past.

step two: the law when you need it

You need not be your own lawyer, but you should be able to converse with one on equal terms

There will be no lawyer jokes in this step. A good lawyer is a gift from the gods. The challenge, though, is finding a good lawyer, just the right one, for you and the work you need to have done. The first two sites below, Lawoffice.com and ABAnet.org, can help you to locate lawyers in different specialties throughout the world. Both sites also give you support in judging whether the match will be a productive one. Lawoffice and the third site in this step, Nolo.com, help you to understand the law. You may choose to work on some problems for yourself, as you develop that understanding, but in any case, a familiarity with the process will help you immeasurably in conversing about important matters with your lawyer.

lawyers and law talk

Lawoffice.com

West Group

Corporate HQ: Eagan, Minnesota

NO CHARGE   ARCHIVE

There are more lawyers in America than people—anyway, it's close. There are 800,000 lawyers and countless firms, and yet finding one can still be tricky, especially in a particular specialty or in a strange city. West Group, a company that publishes legal directories in book form, is responsible for Lawoffice.com, which has a Lawyer Search right on its homepage. Using the search requires nothing more than the designation of a specialty and a city. From the list that results, you can click on certain names or firms for detailed information, and in many cases, you can e-mail a lawyer directly from Lawoffice's site. Since the Lawyer Search also has an international scope, I decided to test it by searching for a sports and entertainment lawyer in a place called Terceira. I found that name on the list of countries: I have never heard of Terceira, but I know one thing about it now. There isn't enough in the way of sports and entertainment to support even one lawyer in the

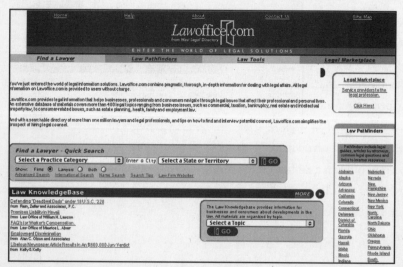

specialty. The Lawyer Search did, however, find four criminal attorneys. Let that say what it will about Terceira.

Lawoffice.com also offers what it calls a Knowledge Base, or a collection of articles submitted by lawyers. The topics are well chosen and can grant at least some perspective on any legal situation you might confront. The titles—be warned that they tend to be witty—are for example, "A Downer for Prozac," "Love, Marriage, Greencards and Divorce," and "Tanks A Lot! Or Lunch at Louie's," which is a fictionalized discussion of contamination codes.

The ABA was founded in 1878 in Saratoga Springs, New York, at a time when that hot town was the Las Vegas of the country, and lawyers were a disorganized lot. It appears that everything has changed since then. The ABA has 400,000 members, and its website can refer you to any one of them, or to a member firm, but only by location. After you designate a state, county, or city, ABAnet will link your search to a local bar association, accordingly. The local organizations typically make referrals only over the telephone, since a certain measure of discussion can help to pinpoint the best match between attorney and client. The General Public button on the homepage can also lead to information on Legal Assistance—low cost or even free counsel, for those meeting income requirements ($9,300 to $18,930, as of this writing). The site features another program, one that has gained popularity in recent years: the Prepaid Law Plan. In many respects, it is a modernized version of the retainer.

Nolo Publishing has grown over the past three decades by promulgating an improbable legal concept: lawyerless law. Its books have helped to educate the public in many of the processes of the law, and its website continues that mission. Whether people then choose to hire counsel or tend to the legal work by themselves, the preliminary groundwork is bound to serve them well.

Bright, without being irreverent, Nolo's site is extensive. Much more than an electronic book, Nolo.com is a prime example

referrals

ABAnet.org
American Bar Association
HQ: Chicago, Illinois

NO CHARGE

Short Shots

Fairmark.com—tax guides aimed at investors and traders
LawyersWeekly.com—"Top Ten Verdicts of the Year," eye-popping accounts of liability suits, from $4.9 billion on down
Legal.gsa.gov—the Federal legal code
1040.com—download any recent state or Federal tax forms

do it yourself

Nolo.com
Corporate HQ: Berkeley, California

NO CHARGE   ARCHIVE   E-COM

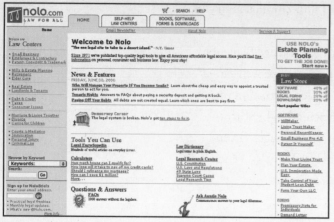

of a site that does, indeed, play upon the power of a website, with both its Legal Encyclopedia and its Dictionary being intelligently annotated with links to related topics. For example, definitions in the Dictionary are linked throughout to sub-dictionaries, so that if a certain term intrigues you, a whole list of similar ones is presented for browsing. The depth of the site's dictionary exploits the power of the Internet in a way that many textual sites cannot.

Another feature of the site is Auntie Nolo, a character who answers legal questions sent by readers. One, for instance, was from a rock musician from the 1970s, whose recordings started selling again; he wanted to know why he wasn't receiving any royalties. Her answer, under the title, "Still Destitute After All These Years," contained pointed advice, including telephone numbers of industry groups that could help.

just one more thing . . .

Patents.IBM.com

IBM Intellectual Property Network

NO CHARGE

SEARCH

ARCHIVE

If you have ever had an idea for a new invention, but had no idea what to do about it, there is hope at last. IBM has created a site that must be the greatest invention ever, because it is, itself, the master of 2,601,705 other inventions.

The site, which does not require registration of any sort, grants access to all of the U.S., Japanese, and European patents of the past 30 years. You type in the name of your invention, and then it tells you if somebody has already patented it. Without, I hope, divulging too much about my own next million-dollar idea (the rest of this sentence is a secure site), I typed in "soap cover," and learned that nothing is covered by a patent in this gaping field! Exploring the possibilities in another of my future realms, I furtively typed in "sneaker," and was given a list of 91 patents. I realized that I had better get moving with my idea, as the field has been well-trodden, so to speak, and so I studied the competition. The first patent on the list described "a sneaker to simulate the sight and sound of a snake."

Link List

FindLaw.com—well-rounded legal offering
TaxResources.com—complete tax links
InfoCtr.edu/fwl—a college project listing every Federal government site, large or small

Patents.IBM.com is not only a site for budding inventors, but for entrepreneurs, as well: It makes a notation next to those patents for which licensing rights are still available. For about $10, you can order a full copy of any patent listed. You can go see for yourself about the sneaker that looks like a snake.

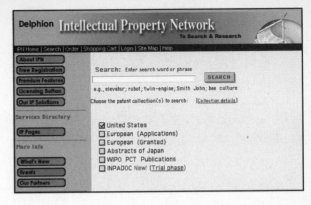

Taxes and Law

The Long and Short of

* One of the easiest ways to get into trouble is by spending your tax money. With investments, people are often tempted to buy something with any profit they have when they sell a stock (or another vehicle). Whenever you realize taxable income, set the portion that you estimate for taxes in a separate bank account—somewhere far from your brokerage account. Then pay it when it is due (usually on the quarter). You should get your tax advice from an accountant or attorney, but always keep in mind that one sure way to stay ahead in taxes is to take good care of the money you owe.

* Lawyers in all specialties thrive on records. When you are involved in any matter that could turn into a case, keep every scrap of paper pertinent to it in a file or envelope, and, furthermore, jot down the details of conversations or other relevant encounters, with dates and even times.

Online brokerages:
taking stock

The course of a trading decision can take many different routes and progress at all different speeds, depending on the online brokerage you choose.

At last count, there are more than 140 online brokerages, with banks and insurance companies just beginning to open trading divisions on the Internet every day. Don't be drawn to one brokerage or another by mere advertising, for the choices range much too widely for that. In fact, online brokerages are about as similar to each other as automobiles. As with cars, there are economy models among online brokerages, offering cheap rates, but little in the way of personal service. There are mid-range brands, with at least a modicum of comfort, and there are also luxury models, giving you the convenience of Internet research and communication, along with the individual advice of a personal broker.

And like cars, the actual features can vary, too, even within a price range. Though all online brokerages can handle stock trades, the ability to trade in mutual funds, bonds, and/or options is not a given, nor is the option of telephone service, with touch tone orders. And just as you might not take a fancy to a certain brokerage, a brokerage may not necessarily take to you, either. Some require minimum account balances, proof of investment experience, or the acquisition of special computer software.

Because the variety in brokerages is presumably equal to the wide range of clients, we can't recommend any particular brokerage, any more than we can advise every reader to go out and buy a red Morgan roadster. An individualized fit is especially important, because your brokerage's limitations will quietly serve to shape your investment predilections. However, by following the two steps below, you should be able to look past the brokerage with the oldest name or the funniest advertising to select the one best suited to your portfolio.

Yahoo! definition

Mutual Fund: An investment pool, the mutual fund offers shares in a large portfolio. The shareholder enjoys two basic benefits: professional management of the portfolio and its diversification among a range of stocks or other financial investments.

Link List

InvestorLinks.com
InvestorMap.com

Yahoo! Quote

After going online, most investors may have become overconfident, which led to a behavior of excessive trading. In short, online investors traded more actively, more speculatively, and less profitably than before.

—From *Wall Street to Web Street: A Report on the Problems and Promise of the Online Brokerage Industry*, the office of the New York State Attorney General [www.oag.state.ny.us/investors/1999 _online_brokers/brokers.html]

step one: choosing a broker
Websites that help you define your needs and match them to a brokerage

Step One contains resources that can be used either to find a brokerage or to keep a watchful eye on the one you already use. The sites listed below help you to shop for an online brokerage, isolating points of comparison and apprising you of both objective facts and subjective impressions. The first two, Xolia.com and ActiveBuyersGuide.com, are interactive, soliciting your predilections and suggesting suitable firms.

stockbroker screener

Xolia.com

Corporate HQ: Oakbrook, Illinois

 NO CHARGE SEARCH CALC.

Xolia.com coined its own expression for online trading, "click'nvesting," which may seem a bit chirpy for an endeavor as portentous as finance. However, the website can offer visitors real support in the selection of an online brokerage, through a process credited on the site to artificial intelligence. Xolia monitors 56 online brokerages and sorts them according to the kind of services they offer. All 56 allow you to trade stocks, but if you indicate that you also want to transact mutual funds, for example, the list shrinks to 45. Add bonds, and the list is cut to 10. In this way, you can watch your priorities cull through the field. Likewise, the results may help you to shape your priorities.

Xolia, a word fashioned from the Latin for "to choose wisely," maintains free-standing lists of brokerages offering real-time quotes, options trading, and short-selling. If you like, you can set up a side-by-side comparison of two or more candidate brokerages, to hone in on the details. The site also provides assistance for those mired in other forms of click'n-decision, if that is what it would be called, by providing a selection system for online banks and credit cards.

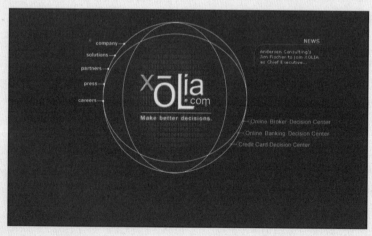

complete advice in broker selection

The ActiveBuyersGuide can help you make an informed choice about purchases, ranging from household control systems to breadmakers. In the same way, the site can help with the selection of an online brokerage—which may be considered a breadmaker, too, of sorts, and a household control system, to boot. The ActiveBuyersGuide will escort you through a series of roughly 10 questions regarding the services that you require in a brokerage and the costs that you are willing to bear. The process is more complex than that of a simple screener, since your answers continually shape the survey as it unfolds. At the end of the survey, the site names online brokerages specifically suited to your needs and personality, detailing their characteristics for you.

Whatever you need, from brokerages to bicycles, the best part of the ActiveBuyersGuide site is the very first step, which always explains each feature or point attendant to a particular buying decision. By the time you understand all of the facets of a decision, the final choice will be easy.

ActiveBuyersGuide.com

Corporate HQ; Burlingame, California

NO CHARGE   SEARCH

examination of brokerages

Donald Johnson, a former professor and a longtime private investor, maintains the Internet's most complete site for the assessment of online brokerage firms. He lists more than 140 in all, sorting them most conspicuously by price per trade: $19.96 to $55; $15 to $19.95, and up to $14.95. After you have a short list of candidate brokerages that are generated by the websites above, take a moment to look them over in the company of Professor Johnson.

Each individual profile includes more than a dozen pieces of necessary data on fees and features, in addition to comments regarding quality of service, contributed by both Johnson and the site's many readers. The site, which is appropriately plain, also offers rankings of brokerages based on either quality or price. The Help in Choosing a Discount Broker feature gives you a choice of 12 different categories with which to match your needs, from firms extending the best margin rates, to those with the lowest account

sonic.net/donaldj

Professor Donald O. Johnson

HQ: Santa Rosa, California

NO CHARGE   ARCHIVE

Yahoo! definition

Futures: In order to make projections regarding costs, producers and end-users of many different commodities rely on contracts, promising the delivery of goods at a specific price at a future date. Because these contracts, known as "futures," can fluctuate in price throughout their specified time span, they attract investors seeking to trade them at a profit.

minimums, to those with no requirements at all. In the general remarks on the homepage, Professor Johnson quotes IBM Chairman Lou Gerstner as saying that an online trade costs a firm all of two cents to execute—a good number to keep in mind as you look for a broker.

locating specialty advisor/brokers

CTA-Online.com
Catonis & Co.
Corporate HQ: Laguna Beach, California

NO CHARGE   E-COM

Properly managed, commodity futures can serve a function even in a relatively conservative portfolio. Improperly managed commodity trading, on the other hand, should be banished to a well-lit corner of the nearest casino.

According to the U.S. government, 90 percent of individuals who invest in commodity futures lose money. And the news gets worse because futures are like the Matterhorn: The view is beautiful from the top, but it's rare to fall only a little way, once you start to tumble. In the past 15 years, Commodity Trading Advisors (CTAs) have sprung up in the financial world, offering investors a vehicle that defrays risk through focused management and the safety of widely based investments. Some CTAs are subsidiaries of banks and other institutions, while some are independent offices. CTA-Online.com ranks CTA's in about 10 ways, including past performance over time-spans ranging from a month to four years. You can order reports and prospectuses on specific firms via e-mail, fax, or post.

step two: sampling the services

A few sites offer tours so that you can see just exactly how online trading works

Just as there are people who hate self-service gasoline stations, there are people who don't care for the sheer work of placing and monitoring trades online. The sites in Step Two allow you to work the buttons. They let you see whether going up and down all by yourself makes you dizzy enough to get off at the mezzanine, or whether the ride feels like a natural. The first pair of sites, from R.J. Thompson and SureTrade, offer demonstrations that require no registration; Merrill Lynch's site has an even better deal, though registration is necessary. The last pair of sites are not exactly brokerages, yet they allow you to oversee practically every step involved in a trade.

One of the rather perplexing things about online brokerages is that so many offer so very little in the way of a thorough, no-obligation demonstration. According to every great salesman, a demonstration is the best sales tool there is, and so it seems odd that, for a mere couple of megabytes of computer gray matter, every online brokerage doesn't produce an irresistible free sample. This book suggests that you take a full tour of those websites that do have detailed demos, in order to familiarize yourself with the basic processes of online trading.

RJT.com, the website of R.J. Thompson Securities, has one of the best-guided tours, showing all of the pages, and prompts you can use to corner General Motors, or at least build a sensible portfolio. The pages cover, in sequence: quotes, orders, portfolios, messages, and overall accounts. SureTrade.com, a low-cost brokerage, uses an animated display to take you step-by-step through the common practices of its trading system.

sampling the wares

RJT.com
R.J. Thompson Securites
Corporate HQ: Omaha, Nebraska

NO CHARGE   E-COM

SureTrade.com
Corporate HQ
Corporate HQ: Lincoln, Rhode Island

a trial run

MLDirect.ML.com

Merrill Lynch

Corporate HQ: New York City, New York

NO CHARGE   E-COM

Merrill Lynch, a full-service brokerage if ever there was one, offers an array of general advice and specific research through its online arm, MLDirect. Among other things, clients receive stock selections through e-mail and can use Merrill Lynch's scanner to search for stocks with certain characteristics. The site can take you on a basic tour through its pages, but it also offers a one-month sample (for which you must register). During your demo month, you receive all of the benefits of an account, except, of course, trading.

bypassing the traditional brokerage

CastleOnline.com

Corporate HQ: Freeport, New York

E-COM

CastleOnline is one of several firms that employs Java software in order to connect you directly to the Nasdaq trading system. The beauty of JavaTrading is the expediency it offers for direct dealings with Nasdaq market makers (firms that match buyers and sellers). Castle neither handles your order, nor participates in it, unlike many online brokerages that fulfill transactions in-house. CastleOnline

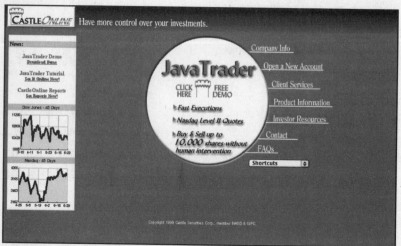

merely escorts your trade through to execution. It features a thorough demonstration of the added benefits and responsibilities of JavaTrading. The demo is informative for any investor as a glimpse of Nasdaq at work. With steep monthly fees that are waived for clients making an average of three transactions per day, CastleOnline is aimed at day traders.

For people with large portfolios, all gains are paper gains, or so it seems. If their stocks soar, they don't go out and buy a yacht—perish the thought. They tell you how much they're worth "on paper," an activity which is obviously more thrilling to them than a summer cruise to the Aegean. For that reason, there is nothing so very virtual about VirtualStockExchange.com, a site that gives you $500,000 in play money and allows you to trade it exactly as the real online brokerages do. It also allows you to bray about it all, just as real investors do: Now, when my friends and relatives sit around talking about their paper gains or losses, I have something to do. I chime in with my own, courtesy of my virtual account.

Aside from the social motivation for having a $500,000 portfolio, even a fake one, VirtualStockExchange.com offers two serious benefits. First, it simulates the actual experience of online trading, making it the best of all demonstrations. If you are thinking of opening an account at an online brokerage, open one at VirtualStockExchange and maintain it until you are quite comfortable. Second, even for those who already invest, either online or with a traditional broker, VirtualStockExchange has an organized array of links, updated daily, for every listed stock. You can find solid information for any stock, relating to insider-trading, competiton, options, technical charting, and much more.

Note: Trades on the VirtualStockExchange cost $29.95 each—but only in virtual money.

VirtualStockExchange.com
Corporate HQ: New York City, New York

NO CHARGE   SEARCH

Short Shots

Money.com/money/broker —(*Money* magazine) survey and reviews of online brokerages, updated annually.
SIA.com/publications— (Securities Industry Association) click on Investor Information; many brochures are offered, including Online Trading Tips
http://SmartMoney.investing. lycos.com/si/brokers/— (*Smart Money* magazine) broker ratings, good thumbnail sketches, but check the date to be sure how current it is.

Online Brokerages

The Long and Short of

* Before shopping for a brokerage, find out about all the possibilities. Know what an online brokerage *can* offer, so that you can draw up a list of the features you really need. Don't forget that your brokerage's limitations are going to be yours, too.

* Don't let the ease of online trading coax you into believing that there is anything easy or off-handed about investing.

* The most common complaint registered about individual brokerages is that communication at times is slow or non-existent. Before opening an account, investigate the plans and back-up plans by which clients contact the brokerage; if possible, check the procedures for yourself, in advance.

* Check fees and procedures on an ongoing basis; brokerages make sudden adjustments that can come as a very rude surprise to clients.

Stock selection:
get the idea

Stock trades may have become easier and less expensive, but finding fresh ideas for stocks to buy is as intriguing as ever. As you hunt for prime stocks, consider the way it will work alongside the rest of your portfolio, not merely how it appears on its own.

There are an awful lot of websites offering stock tips. And that phrase is doubly apt, because a lot of them are awful. Too many act like race course touts, treating stocks like race horses and offering bypassers absolute sure things . . . for a nominal price. Just like touts, many sites have no compunction about including the reasoning behind a tip. Whenever you come across them, though, you might discern the reason for yourself, which is: *The site's owners bought 500 shares yesterday afternoon.*

Nonetheless, all investors need a flow of ideas. More than that, it is advantageous to know why other investors take the positions they do—to follow the logic behind selections and the strategies that accrue from clear thinking. With the steps below, you can do more than watch monkeys throwing their proverbial darts at the stock page, in order to generate a tip. You can trace the thinking behind a tip, and then test it in a more objective setting within the sites described in sections to follow (especially *Company Research* and *Technical Analysis*).

step one: fresh thinking
On Wall Street, the next-best thing to other people's money are other people's ideas

To buy a stock, you have to know its name: That much is certain. There are many ways to get those names, those germs of ideas that later may turn into actual investments. The work you do early on may give you a clear view of the better companies within a particular industry. Well-rounded reading generates an understanding of conditions evolving in favor of certain industries or specific companies,

Insiders' Tour of Yahoo!—Stock Selection
(finance.yahoo.com)

In addition to quotes and daily news regarding every publicly traded stock, Yahoo! Finance offers many timely suggestions for stock purchases. If you have a set of parameters in mind, such as a certain price-to-earnings ratio or a minimum yield, the Stock Screener will suggest issues based on your preferences in eight such fields. To see what is coming in the way of Initial Public Offerings, the IPO page (biz.yahoo.com/ipo/) found under U.S. Markets lists upcoming sales, with news and a profile of each company coming to the market. The page also charts the performance of the best and worst recent IPOs, and lists offerings by industry, underwriter, and company, even those withdrawn before they entered the market. In the Upgrades/Downgrades section under "Research," Yahoo! Finance also records shifts in coverage made by major analysts. Various lists show the stocks which have been upgraded or downgraded as buying opportunities or for which coverage has been initiated.

Many investors follow reports concerning the earnings-per-share of publicly traded stocks. In a section found under Research, Yahoo! Finance covers earnings closely, advising you of upcoming earnings reports and of recent surprises, either above or below estimates.

TIP: Through Yahoo! Broadcast (biz.yahoo.com/cc), you can hear the actual conference calls where companies announced their earnings; recent calls are

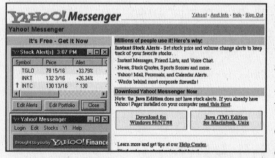

archived, and you can play them back at your convenience. Investors who follow stock splits can find a complete list of them under Reference on Yahoo! Finance. For each stock on the list, the page notes the date of the announcement about the split, and the day on which it is to take place.

TIP: If you are following a particular company, you can use Yahoo! Messenger (messenger.yahoo.com/messenger/stocks.html) to create custom Instant Stock Alerts. One will flash on your screen whenever a designated stock reaches a preset volume, price limit or percentage change.

but don't confine your reading to business publications if you really want the fullest and freshest understanding. The sites below will also open your eyes to ripe stock picks—names. The first ones offer you ideas, along with the reasons behind them, while the last one lets you supply the reasons.

Validea.com
Corporate HQ: Bloomfield,
Connecticut

NO CHARGE   SEARCH

Validea looks for analysts who know what they are doing, and then reports exactly what they *are* doing about stocks. The site follows individuals and companies that claim to foresee the future in stock performance and their every recorded thought. It then does the cruelest thing one can do to any soothsayer: It waits a little while and reports on the outcome. The site establishes an overall pattern of success or failure for dozens of well-known analysts and compiles the results in either of two ways: You can name a stock and find out what has been said about it recently, or you can select an analyst and find out what stocks currently interest him or her (or even it, in the case of a company).

In the hierarchy of Wall Street oracles, the high priests are known as *gurus*. They don't do anything as pedantic as suggesting mere stocks; they suggest a whole system of choosing stocks.

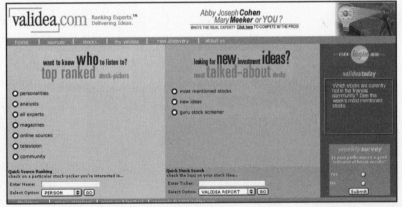

Validea.com has paid nine gurus not money, but the compliment of thoroughly studying their systems. The site pays the rest of us the favor of maintaining lists of stocks presently failing within the recommendations of the various systems. I then took this exercise one step further and looked for that one homecoming king of stocks beloved by the greatest number of gurus. (Thus, I have a system and can now be considered a guru, too.) The site accommodates this kind of a search, though it is rare that even five of the nine gurus agree on one selection.

up-and-coming stocks

Redchip.com
Corporate HQ: Portland, Oregon

NO CHARGE

SEARCH

A blue chip stock, as most people know, is an established security with a steady outlook. A "red chip" is a newer slang that also refers to a well-regarded stock, one representing a medium capitalization company, but as the color red suggests, one with an increased potential for volatility. Redchip.com, dedicated to newer, younger companies, is produced by the editors of a newsletter called *Redchips,* which is known for conducting its own thorough investigation and analysis. Much of the newsletter's proprietary research spills into the site at no cost, although downloads of some reports require a subscription ($99 per year). To look for stock ideas, find the Discoveries section toward the bottom of the homepage, where at least three companies are described each week. Another section, the Reporter, offers company news gathered by site reporters, while the Radar section charts up-to-date red chip movement in the markets. The section called Direct contains an engaging discussion of both Initial Public Offerings (IPOs) and, to coin a new term, Yesterday's Public Offerings (YPOs).

Redchip.com also allows you to hunt around for new ideas on your own in the Research section, where red chip companies are sorted according to sector. For example, there are 56 possibilities listed in the Automobile and Aerospace section, ranked according to your choice of a dozen financial characteristics, such as return on equity or the proportion of shares held by institutions.

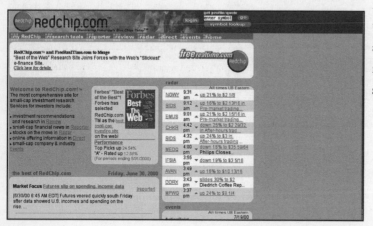

In addition to well-rounded research, WorldFinanceNet.com offers three sections ripe with ideas for stock selection. The first are the Stock Journals, which profile "Good Stocks in Good Industries," the industry sectors being technology, utilities, medical, basic materials, and consumer goods and services. The site suggests at least a dozen "good stocks" in each, with basic information about the company and a tightly written paragraph analyzing the stock's outlook. The second feature, WorldFinanceNet's IPO Corner, is more accessible and engaging than some whole websites devoted to that nervous edge of the stock market. Upcoming offerings are described and so is the prevailing atmosphere—always a factor in the price jumps IPO investors long for. Thirdly, WorldFinanceNet pipes up with what it calls "special situation stocks," which are notably more speculative and time-sensitive than the "good stocks in good industries." The editors only list them as they suggest themselves, avoiding the obligation to list a hot opportunity even when only a lukewarm possibility exists.

Philosophically, one despairs of an investment site with a name that harkens to any kind of jumping. However, 123jump.com is chock-full of news, much of it gathered by in-house reporters, and presented in a responsible way, making it a rarity in both respects for a stock site. So perhaps the name can be overlooked. The site follows Internet and technology stocks as a specialty, featuring the advantage of proportionate overseas reporting. For those looking for new names to place on their long list of possible stocks, 123jump offers a good basic stock screener: Note your requirements in about three dozen areas, and it will generate a list of suitable stocks. Neither the stock screener nor the news segments of 123jump represent the end of a stock search, mind you, but only the beginning.

research and ideas

WorldFinanceNet.com

Corporate HQ: Sarasota, Florida

worldly ideas

123jump.com

Corporate HQ: Miami, Florida

custom search

MarketGuide.com

Corporate HQ: Lake Success, New York

NO CHARGE SEARCH ARCHIVE

"NetScreen" at MarketGuide.com is one of the most vigorous stock screeners on the Internet. In fact, it is actually designed for professional use, and amateurs are well advised to click the Simple Screen box in the upper left hand corner. Even at that, NetScreen offers you a choice of 84 variables by which to whittle down its original list of 9,460 stocks, one step at a time. For example, I specified stocks with a yield greater than 5 percent, leaving 564 possibilities. Requiring that more than 25 percent of the shares be held by institutions left 273, and that the company employ more than 3,000 workers left 87. Specifying a price-earnings ratio of less than 10 reduced the number to 35, while adding that sales growth must be greater than 35 percent left two companies—two companies presumably worth further research [see sidebar].

MarketGuide.com keeps files for research on 13,000 companies, including financial reporting and raw research from the business and public relations newswires. The site watches stocks in the marketplace very closely, too, and the "What's Hot" section on the homepage lets you peruse the big movers in all the different industries, sectors, and stock-price categories.

Adventures With the MarketGuide.com Stock Screener

Taking a rapidly conservative stance where stocks are concerned, I challenged MarketGuide's stock-screening tool to find issues that would do practically everything well, and all at once—established, well-respected companies that would pay a goodly income (or *cash dividend*), while maintaining their own business growth at a fair gallop. I didn't want to lose money on an overly volatile or dull stock. I wanted to make it: four times a year at dividend time, and secondarily, in the potential increase in the stock price.

MarketGuide total field: 9,460 stocks

Specification One: Stocks with a yield greater than 5 percent.

The yield of a stock (or of a bond) is the return in the form of cash dividends. It is calculated by dividing the annual cash dividends by the current stock price. Some stocks, especially those of newer companies, don't pay cash dividends, and so they have no yield at all.

Remaining field: 564 stocks

Specification Two: More than 25 percent of the shares are held by institutions.

Pension funds, mutual funds, and insurance companies are examples of the institutions that make sizable investments in stocks, and which, therefore, can affect corporate governance. Such institutions typically perform indepth research on their holdings. Pension funds, in particular, often prefer stable stocks. These are only tendencies, but a relatively high percentage of stock in the hands of institutions indicates a company of good reputation and outlook.

Remaining field: 273 stocks

Specification Three: Company employment of more than 3,000 workers.

A large company is bound to receive considerable scrutiny and press coverage, while a small one can remain independent of constant observation. Either circumstance can be considered beneficial, but in looking for stability, a larger company is preferable.

Remaining field: 87 stocks.

Specification Four: Price-earnings ratio of less than 10.

The price-earnings ratio equals the price of the stock divided by the annual earnings (which are equivalent to the profit) per share. If it is a high number, the stock has an inflated price, in terms of current results. A high price-earnings ratio of 25 or above reflects, most of all, on the optimism surrounding the stock's future. On a strictly business-like basis, though, without the market and its moods, a lower price-earnings ratio indicates a stock that is worth the price asked—purely as a share of a company making money in its field.

Remaining field: 35 stocks

Specification Five: Sales growth greater than 35 percent.

Sometimes profits can grow even when sales do not—if a company becomes more efficient internally. However, the goal in nearly all businesses is to increase sales, and thus, opportunities for profit. An annual sales growth of about 10 percent is a basic standard for corporate health. In good years, of course, the sky is the only limit on sales growth. Growth of more than 35 percent is hefty enough, though, to show that a company has vigor.

Ending field: Two stocks

Both of the resulting stocks were those of utilities in Texas. Utilities tend to pay a healthy yield, while their growth is attached to that of the general economy in the region where they conduct business.

A good stock screener, such as that of MarketGuide, can extend your education, not only about specific stocks, but about the many considerations that can inform your ongoing decisions about the market.

step two: sample portfolios

The overall composition of your stock holdings is just as important as the names held within

Link List

**Wirehouse.com
StockFever.com**

Yahoo! Quote

I'm often surprised by investors who spend more time deciding what movie they'll rent than on what stock to buy.

—Arthur Levitt, chairman of the SEC, in a speech May 4, 1999
www.sec.gov/news/speeches/
spch274.htm

Never forget that a mess of stocks is like a pile of rubble. Think in terms of the whole portfolio and the way that the strengths of stocks can build upon each other, like bricks in the wall of your house. I doubt that a strong personal portfolio could be built with less than three different stocks, and I believe that one with more than 20 would almost certainly include unnecessary strays, which are hard to watch. No matter how many components you choose, the overall makeup of a stock portfolio is more important in the long run than the individual stocks within it. To continue the analogy to masonry, you can have rock-hard bricks in a wall that crumbles because it's built so badly. The sites in Step Two show all kinds of portfolios and the way that they can serve different purposes. The first describes a diabolically simple stock selection called the Dogs of the Dow, which has proven itself a consistent winner in the past.

a blue chip system

DogsoftheDow.com

Corporate HQ: Long Beach, California

NO CHARGE

"Dogs of the Dow" is the common name for a simple strategy that very often turns in better gains than many of the more tortuous stock systems. It involves taking positions on the 10 highest yielding Dow Jones 30 stocks and maintaining them, come what may, for a whole year. There isn't too much more to it than that, but whatever there is can be found at DogsoftheDow.com, which claims that the theory has turned in an average return of 17.3 percent since 1973. The site shows the stocks that rank as the Dogs of the Dow at the present, and it charts the progress of the theory through each calendar year, since many people initiate their portfolio, according to the theory, on the first of each year. For people who don't want to buy 10 different stocks, or who can't really afford to do so, the FAQ2 section of the site describes how

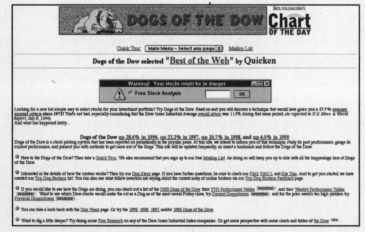

the purchase of Unit Investment Trusts can be utilized in such a case. Finally, the site suggests a variation on the whole idea, which is related to the lowest priced of the 10 Dogs and is called the Puppies of the Dow.

a flock of working portfolios

A private investor in Nashville established the Elf Report and designed the eight portfolios that are tracked on the site. Among them are compilations of speculative stocks, with a seemingly attractive, but uncertain future: "stable growth, large capitalization," of the more predictable large companies, and undervalued stocks, which lag behind their actual worth. Each portfolio is accompanied by a brief outline of the characteristics of the holdings and the goals of the portfolio. The MidCap portfolio, for example, follows, in a general way, the comments of Kenneth Fisher, of *Bloomberg Personal Finance*. It includes medium-size, or middle-capitalization, companies. The editor of the Elf Report ranks the portfolios each week on the basis of annual return; safety, success, and high success. While several of the portfolios tend to under-perform the S&P 500, which is considered a standard average, the site is not supposed to be a recipe followed to the letter. Rather, it is an opportunity to see eight well-considered plans at work, day-by-day and year-to-year.

[no www.]Pages.Prodigy. net/ElfReport

Corporate HQ: Nashville, Tennessee

NO CHARGE

just one more thing . . .

You know the old expression, "If it sounds too good to be true, it probably is." Not everyone heeds it, for money is still cascading into scams of all types. However, perhaps it can be rewritten a bit for this section. If it is a stock, and it sounds even *so-so,* go immediately to StockDetective.com. The site will sober you up in a hurry, unveiling all of the prominent scams at work in the stock world of the Internet. The "Stinky Stocks" list describes specific issues and the outright frauds perpetrated around them, including the "pump 'n dump" game of cheap stocks. In that technique, a group runs up a stock with its own purchases, promotes the surge as widely as possible, and then sells out as soon as inexperienced investors rush in

StockDetective.com

FinancialWeb

Corporate HQ: Orlando, Florida

NO CHARGE   SEARCH   ARCHIVE

where angels fear to tread, pushing the price up for the pump 'n dumpers.

StockDetective, a subsidiary of a research website called Financial-Web.com, also monitors sites that receive payment for promoting particular stocks, and maintains a long list of them. According to StockDetective, one fairly well-known website commented recently on a certain stock, it "... is extremely undervalued! We believe this stock will appreciate substantially from its current valuation ..." As it turned out, the website had been paid $5,000 to feature the stock. Both the name of the stock and the name of the site were plainly revealed on StockDetective.com.

Short Shots

FreeRealTime.com—free instant quotes, registration required
TulipsandBears.com—complex site with extensive data, especially good on emerging market companies and research

Stock Selection

* Keep a notebook in which you can jot down the reasons that you bought a certain stock, held it during adversity, or sold it. Your notebook will become your own best teacher, as you see in plain English what happened and why. If these things aren't set down in writing, they become practically impossible to recollect, amid the swirling changes of Wall Street.

* The composition of your portfolio is more important than any single stock within it.

* You can find ideas for stocks by looking at the holdings of mutual funds that you respect (the holdings are listed in the prospectus; the top 10 holdings are listed in the fund profiles on Yahoo! Finance).   *
Stay away from penny stocks (sometimes known as over-the-counter stocks) until you have several years of successful experience with stocks listed on the major exchanges. Penny stocks are very tricky to research, while listed stocks are not.

* Stay away from day trading until you have a large long-term portfolio, and use strict discipline to earmark only about 10 percent of your investment funds, at most, for day trading. The odds are overwhelming that you will lose your money as a day trader—don't lose your whole fortune.

* Take any stock selection that you make through the steps indicated in chapter on Company Research.

Bonds:
relationships with your money

A bond is of form of debt that is easily traded between investors. Depending on the type of bond, it can be a source of consistent income, a safe and steady vehicle for long-term savings, or a speculative investment, one purchased only to be sold again soon at a higher price.

Common wisdom predicts that you can get rich through stocks, but you can *stay* rich through bonds. As a matter of fact, if you are smart, you can get very, very rich through bonds, too. A bond is a portable form of debt, which can either be kept or sold on the market. In the olden days of the nineteenth century, before banks became prominent, rich people often accepted bonds (sometimes called notes) from individuals, in exchange for a cash loan. Now, the flow of money is quite the opposite. When a large entity such as a corporation or government requires a loan, it turns to the little people (and some large institutional investors, to boot), splintering its desired loan into little pieces called bonds, and letting them circulate. Some people would say that the excitement then stops, as bondholders sit back on a veranda somewhere, waiting for their bi-annual (or monthly) interest checks. While it can work that way, other investors are attracted to the action that surrounds the secondary market for pre-owned, slightly used bonds, where a dozen influences impact on the price of the bond. Read them right and you can make money on the principal and the interest—getting paid for making money, so to speak.

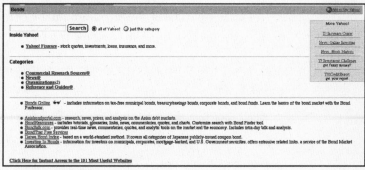

A Guide to Bonds

Corporate bonds (healthy yields on a straightback chair): A company seeking cash can bypass banks and other institutions, selling its debt through bonds that pay a rate of interest largely depending on the stability of the company. Corporate bonds carry the added assurance that should the company fail, the bonds are redeemed by the company before many of its other obligations.

High-yield bonds (corpulent yields on a rickety chair): If a company has no particular stability to brag about, but still needs money to take advantage of opportunities in its business, it can tempt investors by issuing bonds returning a high rate of interest. Sometimes called "junk" bonds, these high-yield bonds are popular with aggressive investors.

Zero coupons (a moneybox for long-term savings): In the old days, you would retrieve your interest payment on a bond by clipping a little coupon right off the certificate every month. In the zero coupon bond, there are no coupons, real or implied. You don't get your interest as regular payments but, rather, agree from the start to let it accrue, while it is compounded all the while. The zero coupon is a boon to any long-term savings plan.

Treasuries (a strongbox for any kind of savings): The U.S. government issues debt in three forms bills, notes, and bonds.

—The minimum for a T-bill is $10,000; all of the interest is paid out at the start, and you may buy it for terms up to one year.

—The T-note has a lower minimum investment, as low as $1,000, but the money must be left in the bond for at least two years. Interest is paid monthly.

—The T-bond has an even longer term, starting at 10 years, and a minimum of just $1,000.

Mortgage bonds (gives that nasty expression "due on the first of the month" a happy ring, one referring to your dividend check): Bonds backed by a single mortgage or a group of them.

Dividend payment: Many bonds are purchased to generate steady income, which arrives in the form of the dividend payment made regularly by the issuer.

> **Tax-free municipals** (do not buy these if you enjoy paying income tax every year!): To encourage people to buy bonds for community development projects, the Federal government does not charge income tax on the interest income from municipal bonds. Depending on the nature of the bond, state, and local income tax may also be waived.

step one: picking a suitable type of bond
Like cards in the deck, each has its strengths

Bonds are issued in a great variety. Stocks, in most cases, require only the basic choice of an underlying company. Bonds carry not only the choice of the issuing entity—which may be a government body, a corporation, or a non-profit institution—but the type of bond, as well. A bond is characterized most noticeably by how and when the interest is paid, and what recourse is offered for early repayment of the bond by the issuing entity (known as the "calling" of the bond). The sites in Step One describe various bonds according to these two dimensions: Who is the issuer and what are the specific features.

┌─ Yahoo! definition ─┐

Securities: A security is a financial vehicle, which can be issued in many forms including stock, which rests on equity (a piece of owner-ship), and bonds, which rest on debt.

overview of a disparate industry

The Bond Market Association is a trade group representing firms associated with all sorts of bonds, and its website offers clear information about practically all types of firms. To ensure that you have not overlooked any of the small points, InvestinginBonds.com offers clear descriptions of each sort of bond, along with an investor's checklist applicable to each bond. Another feature on the site is an explanation of how to read bond prices in the newspaper—should you follow any particular securities every day. If you do follow the market, the site carries basic pricing information on a current basis. In the realm of the tax-free municipal bonds, which are issued by governments and other non-profit entities, the driving force is always the calculation of tax-free versus taxable returns, the dividends not being subject to income tax on the Federal (and sometimes the state or city) level. InvestingInBonds.com has a trustworthy calculator, taking state-of-residence, filing status, and

InvestinginBonds.com
Bond Market Association
Corporate HQ: New York City, New York

NO CHARGE

CALC.

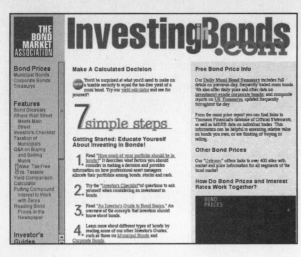

annual income into account, before piping up on the advisability of your buying tax-frees. Some calculators on other sites overlook the state of residence, which can make a big difference in the results.

The best of the introductory sites, Investing-InBonds has a relaxed, unaggressive aura, conducive to bringing people into the world of bond investing, slowly and surely. The website includes an extensive collection of links.

learning about the safest of all investment vehicles

PublicDebt.treas.gov
HQ: Washington, D.C.

NO CHARGE

CALC.

www.savingbond.com
HQ: Milwaukee, Wisconsin

NO CHARGE

CALC.

QUOTES

The biggest debtor in the country *is* the country, despite the fact that, in early 2000, the U.S. government actually cut back on the amount of new debt it was issuing through its popular auctions. You needn't fret, though; it still borrows heavily and tries to do so in a way that lets citizens reap the benefit. Even if it could simply call up one of those kids in Silicon Valley or Seattle and borrow a trillion or so, it wouldn't do so, because extending bonds to a wide body of citizens is also a way of connecting those citizens to their government. The website, PublicDebt.treas.gov, makes it easier than ever for investors to buy bonds, by opening an account for direct purchases of Treasury bills, bonds, and notes. As the site explains, these different instruments vary according to price, maturity, and the means of dividend payment.

The bulwark of family investing for many years was the U.S. savings bond. Though it is issued in amounts as low as $25, it is still a serious form of debt. It ought to be used for more than graduation presents, but there are certain areas of confusion surrounding it, such as the rate of interest and how it moves through the life of the bond. That is unfortunate, since the savings bond has been modernized in the past 10 years, offering better rates and more flexibility than ever before. PublicDebt.treas.gov explains the fine points of various savings bonds (which can be purchased on the site), but a private website, www.SavingsBond.com actually does an even better job of explaining the good ol' savings bond. You can check the worth of old bonds, and explore every nook and cranny of the new ones.

aggressive bond investing

StYo.com
Stone & Youngberg
HQ: Los Angeles, California

NO CHARGE   CALC.   E-COM

High-yield bonds were disparaged as junk bonds when they came into fashion in the early 1980s. They represent debt that is not very highly rated, either because the entity issuing the bond is weak financially, or because the debt is left vulnerable among the obligations of even a healthy company. There can be all sorts of reasons why junk bonds receive a low rating. In any case, even though they must be considered more speculative than high-rated bonds, they are not necessarily more speculative than a good many other choices in the financial spectrum. Stone & Youngberg's website, StYo.com, offers an excellent discussion of high-yield bonds, showing how they can be judged and perhaps used in a portfolio.

step two: getting the picture
Stock activity may reflect a nation's business, but bonds reflect its economy

The "secondary market" refers to the buying and selling of bonds after the first transaction, the one in which a bond was originally issued. While many people purchase bonds and keep them until they mature, quite a few others buy them with an eye toward speculating in price gains on the secondary market. News drives individual bond prices, but so do the shifts in the overall body for interest rates: a constant swaying which is most obviously noted each time the governments raises interest rates. The sites in Step Two contain current news that makes an impact on the secondary market for many kinds of bonds.

bonds day-to-day

Moodys.com

Corporate HQ: New York City

NO CHARGE   ARCHIVE

You can find information about bonds interspersed through any financial newspaper, online or in print, but Moodys.com offers almost nothing but. One of the few exceptions is the About Moodys page, which relates the way that Moodys pioneered the whole business of rating bonds in the early 1900s. The same page also explains the factors that impact a bond rating: factors that any bond investor should understand. The act of buying a bond, after all, is the most vivid rating of them all. The Moodys website is admirably serious in tone. The daily Market Wrap-up, found under Ratings off the homepage, offers depthful commentary on news from an array of sources. At longer intervals, the Economics section offers an overview of trends and the ways that they may influence bond prices. The same section charts yield averages, for bonds of various ratings, over the previous three months. The Moodys site also announces and explains changes in the ratings according to specific bonds—making Moodys.com a valuable resource for company research of all kinds.

┌─ **Yahoo! definition** ─┐

Maturity: No bond is immortal; each one is issued to last a certain amount of time: often 30 years. When the time is up, the bond reaches its maturity. At that time, the issuer has to repay the current bondholder the original loan-amount (face value) of the bond and any interest that has remained in the bond.

supermarket of bond news

BondResources.com

Corporate HQ: Boston, Massachusetts

NO CHARGE   SEARCH   QUOTES   E-COM

The fact that some bank in China is struggling to fight rumors of its imminent demise will probably not affect a municipal bond funding a new playground in Prairie de Chien, Wisconsin. (Though it might; you never know with bonds.) BondResources.com separates the news every day, according to the type of bond it might affect, creating separate pages for Treasury, Municipal, Corporate, International, and Savings. The Economy page carries the usual news flashes generating by every sigh or smile noted on the face of a Federal Reserve governor, but it also picks up those smaller news stories that can presage economic trends: the price of gasoline, for one. Most of the news on BondResources.com including its many charts, is culled from other sites. While the site does not sell bonds, it does

┌─ **Yahoo! definition** ─┐

Collateralized Mortgage Obligations (CMOs): A form of security that bundles mortgage bonds and pays interest accordingly.

have an effective bond-finder, so that you can locate the exact securities in which you are looking to investigate.

step three: trading floors
These are sites that welcome those who are "just looking"

Every full-service brokerage underwrites, or agrees to distribute for sale, an inventory of various new bond issues. In addition, most brokerages, even discount houses, can handle the purchase and sale of bonds on the secondary market. A handful of brokerages specialize almost exclusively in the world of bond trading. Step Three offers two sites that are charting new territory by promoting free-standing sources for bond sales on the Internet.

┌─ **Link List** ─────────┐
BondsOnLine.com
MoneyPages.com/syndicate
└──────────────────────────┘

checking out new bonds

You can actually purchase bonds through the Tradebonds.com site. More importantly, though, the company allows considerable research and perusal of its inventory even without registration. Sifting through actual issues can be a valuable education, especially when the range of categories is as wide as it is on Tradebonds, covering treasuries, corporates, municipals, Collateralized Mortgage Obligations (CMOs), and even non-bonds such as certificates of deposit. Each issue is fully described on a detail sheet. The site's information constitutes a good test: Once you understand all of the figures included on a Tradebonds detail sheet, you might very well be ready to buy bonds anywhere.

Tradebonds.com
Corporate HQ: Newport Beach, California

NO CHARGE | CALC. | QUOTES | E-COM

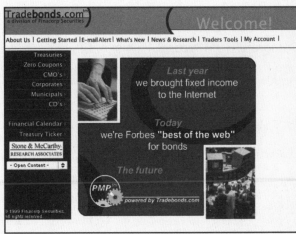

bidding for bonds

muniAuction.com

Corporate HQ: Pittsburgh, Pennsylvania

NO CHARGE   E-COM

Short Shots

www.app.NY.FRB.org/sbr
(Federal Reserve Bank, New York City)—savings bonds

The idea of placing a bond auction on the Internet is a potent one, giving issuers the largest possible customer base and customers an unobstructed view of the field. While the Treasury Department allows Internet account holders to participate in auctions, they can't actually place bids, but, instead, tag along on the bidding of larger players. At MuniAuction, though, pre-approved clients can place their own bids over the Internet during a real-time auction that usually lasts about a half hour. The system is quite simple, with several weeks' advance notice for each auction. Registration is free, and you can prepare thoroughly before participating with real money in a real auction. First, a registrant can bid in moot auctions for practice. Next, he or she can have access to an actual auction as an observer. Once the registrant has expressed an interest in doing some real bidding, MuniAuction will consider the request, and then, at its discretion, grant the necessary access codes.

Even those disinclined to buy municipal bonds ought to take note of the simplicity and power of MuniAuction, which is pushing the frontier of Internet finance in a way that could turn even today's hotshot Internet brokerages into antiques.

just one more thing . . .

DCRCO.com

Duff & Philips Credit Rating

Corporate HQ: Chicago, Ilinois

NO CHARGE   SEARCH

Yahoo! definition

Certificates of deposit (CD): In exchange for the commitment of funds for a set time-period, banks and other financial establishments are often willing to pay an increased rate of interest over that of standard savings accounts. Bank issued CDs are insured by the Federal Deposit Insurance Corporation (FDIC).

Let's just say you don't really know much about accounting, electricity, agriculture, Oklahoma, and—simultaneously—construction. But let's say you want to buy a bond issued by a utility for a new power plant in the middle of the wheat fields of western Oklahoma. Ratings services such as Moodys, Standard & Poor's, and Duff & Philips (which is the sponsor of DCRCO.com) have specialists who know about all of the above disciplines, and a good many more, and they can assess the risk hidden in each aspect of a project or entity connected with a bond issue. The resulting opinion is published as a grade, which is communicated in different ways at each ratings service. However, in any language an "A" is good, and the more of them, the better. If you want to check a rating for a specific issue, Duff & Philips' website is easy to navigate, with ratings for thousands of bonds of all types. Furthermore, in explaining the rating system, the site indicates many of the considerations that affect the perception of a bond's

Bonds

* You can buy bonds for your personal account or through a mutual fund. Either way, though, you must familiarize yourself with the type of bond that best suits your needs.

* You can buy government debt—Treasury bonds, bills, and notes—direct from the U.S. Office of the Public Debt, or through many banks and brokerages.

* One of the most popular types of bonds is the tax-free bond, often known as a "municipal," even when it has been issued by some other form of government or institution.

* No Federal income tax is levied on municipal bonds. No state or local taxes are levied, either, on issues specially qualified by geographic area.

* Not every online or discount brokerage engages in the bond market.

Mutual funds:
safety in numbers

Mutual funds offer an investor the combination of expert management with the chance to take part in a wide range of investments for the price of a single share. Mutual funds were initially intended to be a conservative way for small investors to spread their risks thinly over a market. As this market expanded, the mutual fund manager's expertise in certain sectors became more important to the success of a fund. There are now three main categories of mutual funds: stock funds (also called equity funds), bond funds, and money market funds.

According to the Investment Company Institute, which was formed in 1940 and began following mutual funds before most people had even heard of the term, more than $7 trillion is invested in mutual funds in this country today. There are now *8,300 mutual funds* to choose from, a significant number, considering that there are almost as many stocks being traded on all of the major exchanges. Ironically, mutual funds were invented in the early 1930s to give people one simple choice among investments. In 1940, there were less than 50 funds altogether; today there are more than 50 major *sectors*. In each one, at least 100 separate funds jostle for attention. That doesn't even include the miscellaneous funds, such as the kind that invests only in companies that advertise on NASCAR racing cars.

The steps in this chapter will help you to choose a sector, and then a handful of specific funds that bear the potential to strengthen your portfolio. After that, you might be ready to buy. Oddly enough, the great flaw in the way that people handle their mutual funds is not usually found at the buying end, but at the selling end. Nearly everyone falls into one of two categories that are covered in the first two steps: hanging on to a fund no matter what, even if it under-performs the average potato bug; or selling funds pell-mell, every time one does not out perform the moon. There is

Yahoo! definition

Sectors: Mutual funds are often separated into sectors, according to investment objective—the type of assets a fund holds and/or the way that success will be measured.

Insiders' Tour of Yahoo!—Mutual Funds

At Yahoo! Finance, just about every mutual fund offered in the market is profiled, and you can also find quotes, order prospectuses, and review daily financial news. Yahoo! Finance also lists the top performers in a number of categories, over various time spans.

Under Mutual Funds, in the U.S. Market section of Yahoo! Finance, you can use a mutual fund screener to help start the selection process. **TIP: Don't fill in all eight fields at once, or you may close yourself off from some good prospective candidates. Start with the two or three fields that matter most to you.**

To learn more, take the suggestions generated by the fund screener to the Fund Index under the Reference section, which offers details on every fund operating in America. **TIP: Clicking Profile gives you essential information about a fund, from past returns to fees and expenses.**

Another way to locate the right funds for you is to look at Top Performers, which are listed by investment category and updated daily. Alternatively, you can browse all the funds issued by the same firm through the Funds by Family index.

TIP: If you want to stay right up-to-the-minute on mutual funds, the News section on Yahoo! Finance's Mutual Fund page carries the latest developments from a wide range of news sources.

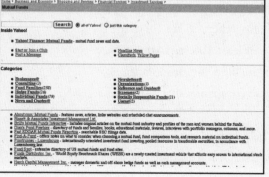

NO CHARGE

SEARCH

CALC.

no recommended time span you should work to remain supple in your attitude toward the mutual funds that you own. Step Three contains sites that can help you to keep an eye on your funds, and on yourself, in that regard.

step one: dissecting the sectors
The right fund will match your needs in all kinds of markets

Although it is perfectly reasonable to sink all of your money in one mutual fund and enjoy the safety that comes with diverse investments, most people today take advantage of specialized management expertise in a wide range of funds, creating their own diversity out of that variety. The first step in creating a portfolio of mutual funds is probably the hardest: looking carefully at yourself. Some of the features you should determine before investing in mutual funds are: your savings goals and timeline, your need for current income, your tax situation, and your ability to withstand losses. Sometimes the type of work you do makes a difference; if you are in a stable career with little chance of unemployment, then your investments may be more aggressive than those of a person in a more precarious career. In addition, the stage of your career is a consideration. For example, it is a good idea to place money, any amount of it, into safe investments in the earliest stage of your career to make the most of compounding your interest.

Before trying to select a specific fund, make sure that you understand what the mutual fund industry is all about as a whole. Explore the investment expectations from which fund categories are carved, for example, and uncover the hidden costs that might affect your actual returns. Learning these things before you purchase is free; learning them after you have purchased a fund may prove to be more expensive. The three sites in this step work well together: The Investment Company Institute supplies a grounding in fund categories and the many other choices facing shareholders. The Mutual Fund Education Alliance helps paint the bigger picture of using mutual funds together in a custom portfolio. Finally, the Securities & Exchange Commission will try to make you as smart as the most clever ad writer at the most aggressive mutual fund company.

Yahoo! definition

Expense ratio: The fees extracted by the mutual fund company, expressed as a percentage of total assets: usually it lies between 0.5 percent and 2 percent.

Yahoo! definition

Front-end sales charge (or "load"): The percentage of a mutual fund purchase taken as a commission at the outset. The sales charge can also be taken on the backend, at the time a customer sells shares in the fund.

introduction to the industry

ICI.org
Investment Company Institute
HQ: Washington, D.C.

NO CHARGE

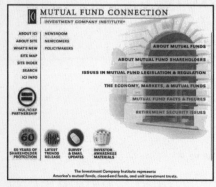

ICI.org, produced by a trade association for the mutual fund industry, starts its Investor Awareness section off with a quiz. The 20 questions range through the types of funds, the precise charges inherent within them, and even the tax implications of different mutual funds. It is a good start, because mutual funds have a way of fostering pockets of ignorance. For example, did you know that more French citizens own mutual funds than any other nationality except Americans? (Now the quiz has 19 questions.) As you go through the quiz, you are offered links to other parts of the site for more information. The Investor Awareness section settles down to business with a series of brochures that can be downloaded to your computer, on such subjects as "Questions You Should Ask" about any mutual fund, and complete information on that serpentine world of mutual-fund fees.

cases for comparison:

MFEA.com
Mutual Fund Education
Alliance
Corporate HQ: Kansas City,
Missouri

NO CHARGE

SEARCH

CALC.

ARCHIVE

When mutual funds were invented, the idea was to buy a fund and keep it, that is why sales charges, called "loads," were exacted at the beginning: If you held the fund for five, 10 or 20 years, the load would be amortized into a pittance. Lately, though, investors have taken to buying and selling stocks after only a few weeks or months—or hours. For that and other reasons, the "no-load" fund has appeared on the scene as a bargain, typically making up the lost sales charge in a continuing higher management fee.

The Mutual Fund Education Alliance represents no-load funds and promotes them throughout much of its website. Even with that as a filter, the site is still worthwhile. However, the Model Portfolios section is especially helpful, and is recommended for people looking to pinpoint the type of funds they require. MFEA.com offers portfolios for a range of simplified investor profiles ranging from Young Professionals to Empty Nesters. Even more useful to you is the chart called, Selecting Funds for

Your Portfolio, with which you can see eight types of investment goals alongside suggested sectors, and rankings for potential risk, income, and appreciation.

Whatever the sector, there are costs and hidden costs involved in the purchase of a mutual fund, and they don't often get the 64-point headline treatment in the newspaper advertisements you see everywhere. The Securities & Exchange Commission's website makes the information, otherwise relegated to the fine print, accessible. The SEC explains a half dozen considerations that many individual investors overlook when plunging into a mutual fund. Among them are: sales charges, fees and expenses, taxes, and the age or size of the fund. The same page is connected by link to a truly marvelous tool, the Commission's Mutual Fund Cost Calculator. As it boasts, the calculator "quickly answers questions like this: 'Which is better, a no-load fund with yearly expenses of 1.7 percent or a fund with a front-end sales charge of 3.5 percent with yearly expenses of .90?' " Have your prospectuses ready, and the calculator will tell you what the headlines never do.

don't be naïve

**www.sec.gov/consumer.
mperf.htm
Securities & Exchange
Commission**
HQ: Washington, D.C.

NO CHARGE

step two: the best of all possible funds
Narrowing the choice to a few mutual funds that are going in the right direction

There are so many mutual funds available these days that there is no reason to choose one that is not stellar. To make sure your selection has the dimension it needs to stand up to the future, you should have at least three good, sharp reasons for investing in any mutual fund. If nothing else, these criteria may force you to look beyond any one, over-arching consideration. To help you to learn to weigh the attractions of mutual funds, the following four sites are listed in the order of the amount of editorial commentary regarding selection. The first, from *Forbes* magazine, offers an intelligent, wide-ranging discussion, along with suggestions, while the last, FindaFund, profiles funds and helps you to contact them.

Yahoo! Quote

If you invested $10,000 in a fund that produced a 10 percent annual return before expenses and had annual operating expenses of 1.5 percent, then after 20 years, you would have roughly $49,725. But if the fund had expenses of only 0.5 percent, then you end up with $60,858—an 18 percent difference.

—From Scrutinize the Fund's Fees and Expenses (www.sec.gov/consumer/mperf.htm)

---

intelligent perspective on selection

Forbes.com
Forbes magazine

Corporate HQ: New York City, New York

NO CHARGE   SEARCH   CALC.   ARCHIVE

Forbes magazine has the reputation of seeing the business world in its own particular way, and the mutual fund section of its full-service site parlays that unique perspective into a refreshing advantage for those interested in finding funds. Drawing material from its magazine, *Forbes* offers an "Honor Roll" of funds in an array of sectors, chosen not merely for past performance, but for the more subtle implications of holdings and management. In particular, *Forbes* tries to assess a fund's likely response to current and developing conditions in the markets. The site also offers a fairly simple fund-finder that reflects your choice from a list of about 100 sectors.

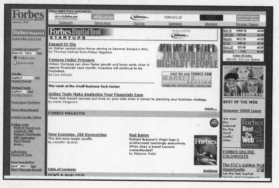

dream up a fund

InvestmentDiscovery.com

Corporate HQ: Philadelphia, Pennsylvania

The most over used criterion for mutual fund selection is past performance. Obviously, it should be of some interest; however, it should be your sole concern only if you earnestly believe that the next year, three years, or five years are going to replicate the past performances in every respect. As with *Forbes*, InvestmentDiscovery.com tries to add another point-of-view to the process of mutual fund selection. Its Funds4U tool invites visitors to list stocks that they like, and the site will then list mutual funds sharing that basic outlook. A free registration is required to use Funds4U and other fund-finding tools on the site. InvestmentDiscovery.com was started by a private investor, and it is one of those sites (see FundAlarm.com) that illustrate the contributions that individuals can add to the financial world through the web.

> ### Yahoo! definition
>
> **Fund manager:** The portfolio activity of a mutual fund is directed by a manager, on whom the ultimate responsibility for the fund's performance falls.

superior ratings service

Morningstar.com

Corporate HQ: Chicago, Illinois

NO CHARGE   SEARCH   CALC.

The Morningstar homepage is lined with stories about stocks, markets, and mutual funds—any of which might influence your next decision to buy or sell. The site's Funds section is even more pointed, of course, with specific picks and profiles for those ready to go—but unsure of exactly where. The section includes a fund-screener that is grounded with about a dozen fields for consideration. Since Morningstar is known more as a rating service, the screener allows you to denote the number of stars, out of five, that would be acceptable to you in a fund.

connecting to a fund company

FindaFund.com

NO CHARGE   SEARCH

A benefit of purchasing mutual fund shares is that they can be ordered directly from the fund company, obviating at least some brokerage charges. FindaFund has a simple website, through which you can locate initial information on any fund, searching either by name or sector, and then contact the fund company for a prospectus and purchase information. Rankings and advice are minimal on the site. However, once you do hone in on a fund through the steps above, FindaFund offers an easy way to learn the toll-free numbers for its fund family.

step three: news and moods
Even in a long-term investment, it behooves you to stay current

Half the idea of buying a mutual fund is that you don't have to worry so much about the day-to-day market pressures on a portfolio. However, the other half of owning a mutual fund is nothing but worry: about the fund, its management, its direction, and its viability under current conditions. Very few investments absolve you of the necessity to worry, at least a little. The first site in this step, Fund

Alarm, helps to keep you up-to-date by taking a steely-eyed view of mutual funds, while the second, Mutual Funds Interactive, tends to be rather more enthusiastic. Both are full of news specific to the world of funds, and you can choose the one that suits your own attitude (or contradicts it, for added strength).

tough on funds

FundAlarm.com
Roy Weitz, CPA and Esq.
HQ: Los Angeles, California

NO CHARGE

SEARCH

Roy Weitz, who created FundAlarm.com, is still fond of a remark made by a journalist who observed that the site does not carry any advertising from companies within the mutual fund industry—and probably couldn't get any if it tried. FundAlarm is not opposed to the whole industry; however, it is outraged by certain fund managers who perennially survive their own ghastly results. The site follows about 3,500 mutual funds and lists those that have consistently underperformed their respective benchmarks (sector averages) over one, three, and five years. Weitz calls those "Three-Alarm Funds," and they are grouped by sector. The first one on the first list, supposedly a growth fund, vastly underperformed the S&P over each time-span; it lost a lot of ground even in 1999, one of the most bullish years for growth stocks. What is really shocking, though, is that this same fund still holds $68 million in investor capital. That point belies the reason for FundAlarm.com: As long as there are people satisfied with mediocre performance, there will always be fund managers willing to provide it.

On the positive side, FundAlarm also ranks "No Alarm" funds, which pass the test by outperforming their benchmarks over the three time spans. Mixed in with the alarms and pleasant silences of "No Alarms," Weitz provides very witty, topical commentary about the world of mutual funds, updated at the beginning of each month. "FundAlarm" is a one-man operation, and since that one man (Weitz) also has a day job, the once-a-month updates can be considered a heroic effort.

Brill.com is solely dedicated to the world of mutual funds, and the editorial section anchored on the homepage contains related features, commentary, and tidbits from the newswires. There are departments devoted to special considerations, such as IRA investing and tax advisories, along with a regular feature that charts the proclamations of newsletters and mutual fund gurus. The site also gives considerable space to tracking the careers of star-fund-managers, an aspect of fund purchases that is receiving more attention than ever these days. Another area of note is the Toolshed, which allows you to research funds and sectors according to a variety of criteria.

news galore

Brill.com

Mutual Funds Interactive;

Corporate HQ: West Boylston, Massachusetts

NO CHARGE SEARCH CALC.

just one more thing...

Amex.com

American Stock Exchange

HQ: New York City, New York

NO CHARGE CALC.

The American Stock Exchange recently copied the mutual-funds' recipe for success, proposing that since mutual funds own stocks, stocks could own stocks, too. The exchange, itself, devised issues that trade exactly as stocks do, but which represent a basket, or portfolio, of other equity stocks. Foremost among them are "Diamonds" issues, which replicate the holdings of the Dow Jones Industrial Average, as one example, or the Nasdaq 100, the Standard & Poor's 500, and so forth, among the well-known indices. In addition, the Amex offers its—would the term be "mutual stocks?"—representing a general mix within nine different sectors, respectively, including tech stocks and utilities.

For those who remain loyal to mutual funds, IndexFunds.com (Austin, Texas) offers a treasure trove of information, including the simple and sophisticated ways index funds can be used in a portfolio. In fact, IndexFunds.com is an engaging site for anyone who would like to fully understand the way that indices form something of a skeleton for the rest of the mammoth market.

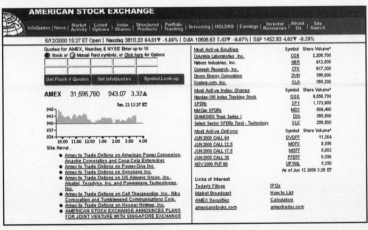

Mutual Funds

* Before you look for the right fund, look for the right category. Know what you need a fund to do. ("Make money" isn't specific enough.)

* Once you have designated the categories you need, compare funds against each other only within each category.

* Past performance is only one way to judge a fund. In considering which to buy, take into account the kind of fund it is and the complexity of the economy over the same span.

* Calculate the effect of fees and expenses on your mutual fund investment.

* Remain well informed about your funds. Investment priorities should be long term—but that doesn't mean keeping disappointing funds long term.

Company research:
pursuing the likely candidate

The easiest way to make a bad investment is to be ill informed. To judge a company effectively, look far past the numbers of Wall Street, and find out everything you can about what a company really does.

There are many reasons to research a company. One is that you may want to invest in it. Another is that you may want to do business with it. You may want to work for it. You may even find yourself living next to it, and want an inkling about what is going on inside. While altogether too many of the Internet's websites offer investment data, information that is constantly distracted by share-price must never be confused with *company research*. This section, then, is devoted to much broader questions of business practice. The steps are meant to locate companies in a certain industry or sector, gain a balanced view of them, and then hone in on the basic nitty-gritty. The irony is that, while this information is directed at the wide array of goals described above, it is probably most important of all to potential investors, who too often ignore anything that can't be expressed in terms of ticks.

Yahoo! definition

Ticks: The incremental amounts by which securities go up or down in value throughout the trading day are called "ticks." For years, a tick has been expressed as a fraction of a dollar, typically ranging from $1/16$th on up. However, some exchanges will soon adopt decimal ticks, expressed in pennies.

step one: locating companies
Finding out who's doing what

The sites in this step can be used for many business purposes in addition to providing information for investors. Individuals or businesses looking for suppliers can search according to product or location, in addition to the company's name. Entrepreneurs considering a new business can learn the lay of the land within a certain field, and in a certain region. For anyone, though, including investors, these sites are a source for basic information about thousands of companies, from start-ups to globals.

Short Shots

CompanySleuth.com—promises aggressive information on companies; results are often tepid, but well-organized, in any case.
IBM.com/investor.financial guide—general resource on how to read company statements and annuals reports
AnnualReportService.com—free mailings

Insiders' Tour of Yahoo!—
Company Research

Yahoo! Finance offers profiles of more than 31,000 issues, including both stocks and mutual funds. Found under Reference on the homepage, the Profiles section of the Company and Mutual Fund Index is an excellent starting point for company research. In addition to a company's Statistics at a Glance, the page includes a description of its business, address, officers and their salaries, and links to company websites. In addition, you can find information on insider and mutual fund holdings in the company, its recent SEC filings, and analysts' upgrades or downgrades of the stock. Whatever information is not found within the profile is very likely to be found through a link on the same page.

Under Financial News, on the Yahoo! Finance main page, you can get news on any company from more than 20 sources, including AP Wire, Reuters, S&P, CBS Marketwatch, Upside, Red Herring, ZDNet, CNet, On24 (audio

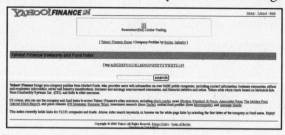 and video), The Street, Worldly Investor, Individual Investor and Industry Standard.

NO CHARGE   SEARCH

background on companies large and small

ThomasRegister.com
Corporate HQ: New York City, New York

NO CHARGE   SEARCH

Name a product or service, and ThomasRegister.com will tell you who provides it in this country or Canada. No widget is too arcane: The site lists 64,000 product headings. For example, let's say you decide to bottle your renowned recipe for wild beach plum jelly. Other than a wild beach on which to find the plums, you are going to need jars, and ThomasRegister lists 25 different kinds, from vacuum to cosmetic to condiment. Under your basic glass jar listing, there are 82 suppliers or manufacturers listed. All told, the site holds information on 156,000 private and public companies in the United States. For each, a basic data sheet includes a description of the size and financial strength of a company, along with contact numbers. The site offers means of gathering even more information, including catalogs for many of the companies.

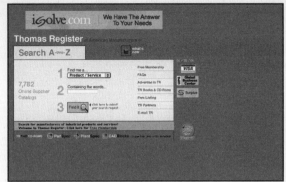

A Short Guide: What to Look for in a Company

Background

* **How does the company make money?** That is not always the same as "What does the company make (or do)?" Some firms generate the biggest part of their profits through silent activities, such as extending credit or licensing patents.

* **Who else is doing the same thing?** Learn all about two or three main competitors and try to talk yourself into buying stock in one of them, instead of your original choice. What differences does the comparison point out?

* **What are the managers like?** Find out who they are, how and when they came to the company, and whether they run the company in a way that you consider advantageous.

Numbers

* **Price/Earning ratio** The price of a share of stock divided by the earnings per share; the lower the resulting number, the better. Traditionally, this is considered a measure of whether or not a stock is overpriced, but a high P/E ratio can sometimes indicate that people are buying the stock based on future earnings potential.

* **Earnings per share** Look over the figures for the past five years; have the earnings come in on a consistent plane? If not, what events affect the company's ability to bring in profits? One case that always requires further investigation is the company that has an increase in sales and a decrease in profits.

* **Yield** Expressed as a percentage, the yield is the rate at which cash and other dividends have been returned in the past year. In most stocks, the yield is somewhat lower than that of bonds.

Future

* **Product flow** What is the product cycle, or the time it takes to plan and produce a new item? How does it compare with that of its competitors? How many new products are scheduled for introduction in the coming year? If the company is not in manufacturing, then translate the theme of these questions accordingly.

* **What is the percentage of revenues devoted to Research & Development (R&D)?** In the short term, R&D may be a drag on earnings, but over the long term, no company can afford to shirk it.

* **How is the company positioned to take advantage of international opportunities?** If the question is applicable (and there are precious few industries unaffected by globalism), then a plan should be in place that you can use in your evaluation.

trademark registrations

USPTO.gov
United States Patent and
Trademark Office
HQ: Washington, D.C.

NO CHARGE   SEARCH   ARCHIVE

The process of registering a trademark is a bit demanding, as well it should be, for some people would trademark the whole English language and then charge the rest of us for talking if the government were not careful about issuing registrations. However, USPTO.gov is not included in this section for the purpose of helping you take out a trademark (though it can do that). Rather, it is here because the trademark search tools on the site offer a cunning opportunity for company research: finding out who has entered a certain field in the recent past. On the homepage, select Searchable Databases on the left and use the tool labeled Combined Marks Search. If you type in some specific product or service, you will see a considerable list of companies that entered the field, along with contact information and a picture of the trademark that they registered.

CommerceInc is working hard to amass what it calls "supplier cards" on every business in the country. The supplier card has information generated from databases, but available for editing by the companies themselves. As the website develops into the anticipated resource, the effort is being paid for by advertising. Intended as a business-to-business resource, CommerceInc.com allows you to search through company profiles, starting with only a website, telephone number, or other bit of information. You can also designate a particular industry, nationwide or within a specific locale, and see who's there. Searching for dart boards, for no particular reason, I found 48 companies. Trying something more difficult, I searched for "cricket," as in the English sport, and found 14 American companies willing to deck me out in whites.

short profiles

CommerceInc.com
Corporate HQ: New York City, New York

NO CHARGE   SEARCH

step two: information if you please
Just knowing the name of a company isn't nearly enough

The sites in Step Two offer in-depth information on publicly-held companies. It comes in varying forms: Hoovers.com, for example, is strongest in the short articles it originates to profile companies, while the Securities & Exchange Commission at SEC.gov grants access to accounting statements and other data, submitted by every public company in the country, according to requirements. The sites below are neither prying nor analytical: They merely allow you to look at company portraits drawn in detail.

Link List

CorporateInformation.com— now part of Wright Investors Service, this is one of the stellar links sites on the web: neatly organized and very sensibly written.
DotcomDirectory.com—(Network Solutions) company finder with special expertise in Internet locales

worldwide reports

http://WISI.com
Wright Investors Service, Inc.
Corporate HQ: Milford, Connecticut

NO CHARGE   SEARCH   E-COM

Wright Investors Service manages several mutual funds and is growing by leaps and bounds as a provider of company research on the Internet. On the homepage, go to Research on the lower left, and hit Company Reports, and you will be rewarded with a torrent of them. You can search by name, ticker symbol, or industry, thereby receiving a report that includes a company profile, research report, and analyses of sales, earnings, and stock price. Wright doesn't limit itself to domestic companies: You can name almost any country and see reports on companies doing business there. Check New Zealand, for example, and there are about three dozen reports to choose from, including Colonial Motor Corp ("18 Ford dealerships from Kaitaia to Ivercargill"). The information is as in-depth for overseas companies as it is for American firms. And, suddenly, you may find yourself asking, "Why is Colonial Motor's stock price down, even though they sell so many cars from Kaitaia to Ivercargill?"

official filings

www.sec.gov
U.S. Securities & Exchange Commission
HQ: Washington, D.C.

NO CHARGE   SEARCH

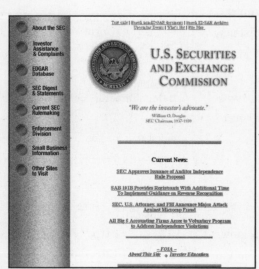

Every corporation has stock, but usually it just sits in a file somewhere, while those few people who own it concentrate on building the business. Once in while they sell their stock, most often to each other. However, as soon as the stock is placed in the public market, represented by brokers and handled by strangers, the Securities & Exchange Commission requires regular filings of financial reports. These SEC filings are a legal necessity, and they are consulted by analysts and investors as indicting the clearest picture of a company's situation. Through the SEC's website, you can search for a company by name, though you will also be asked for the type of form you need, and so it behooves you to look at the explanation of the forms and their coded names on the site. You can look at annual and quarterly reports, prospectuses, and about a dozen other types of filings.

Mutual funds also fall within the domain of the SEC, and searching for information pertinent to them is especially easy, with the Exhaustive Mutual Funds Search, found at the bottom of the homepage. It offers a menu of funds, and asks for a time span (choose "last one month" for the quickest results and most up-to-date information). Keep in mind that whenever you are researching a mutual fund with a purchase in mind, SEC.gov lets you see the prospectus instantly.

Hoovers was started about a decade ago by a gaggle of University of Chicago alumni, and it has grown into a reliable source of company profiles, both on the Internet and in reference books. There is no charge on the website for a basic snapshot of a company, which includes a one-paragraph description, officers, and financial statistics. Most of the same information can be found at SEC.gov, if the truth be told, but Hoovers.com makes it much more accessible and even appealing. The description of Whirlpool, for example, begins rather breezily, "With a brand name recognized by anyone who ever separated dark colors from light, Whirlpool is the world's #2 producer of major home appliances . . ." For those who require more extensive information than the snapshots can deliver, the site offers a membership at $109.50 per year, which unlocks further information.

Hoovers.com

Corporate HQ; Austin, Texas

NO CHARGE   SEARCH   E-COM

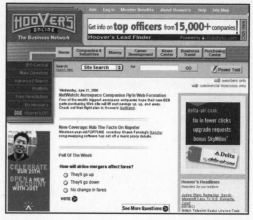

step three: private investigations

Run a company through all of these sites to paint an even bigger picture

If you want or need to know more about a company than what is in its press releases, Step Three lists sites that shine a light into all the dark corners where the dirt lies. The results emanate from the experience of knowing exactly where to look. Each of these sites concentrates on a different area, from environmental pollution at Scorecard.org to securities manipulation at Securities.Stanford.edu. These sites are neither gullible, nor easily satisfied. At each, you will find a flinty-eyed person holding the flashlight, inspecting American business.

Yahoo! definition

Federal Trade Commission (FTC): The U.S. agency that regulates business markets to ensure that consumers have fair choices and that companies conduct themselves in a way that does not restrict competition.

misconduct in stocks and other investment vehicles

According to a judgment handed down in a Northern California court, all SEC legal activity must be available to the general public via the Internet. Stanford University's law library volunteered to set up online access to the SEC's legal files, and the resulting site enables you to search for class action suits filed by the shareholders of any publicly-held company. For example, a case chosen at random

http://Securities.Stanford.edu
Robert Crown Law Library, Stanford University
HQ: Palo Alto, California

NO CHARGE   SEARCH   ARCHIVE

advised that "... complaint alleges that the company disseminated false and misleading information about its financial results ... as a result, the company stock traded at artificially high share prices." If you were considering the purchase of shares in that company, wouldn't you want to know more about the suit? That is the very purpose of Securities.Stanford.edu.

behavior in the marketplace

FTC.gov
Federal Trade Commission
HQ: Washington, D.C.

NO CHARGE   SEARCH   ARCHIVE

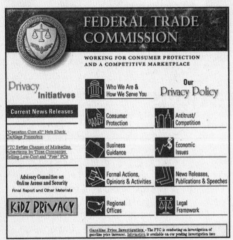

Another government site that keeps track of naughty companies, whether they are publicly held or privately owned, is FTC.gov. The Federal Trade Commission is vitally concerned with misdeeds in the marketplace, from attempts at monopolization to false advertising. If you type in the name of a company, you will see the entire content of the FTC's file on that company, though I have to add a disclaimer of sorts. The file will include appearances, hearings, and conference remarks that are not related to any sort of problem or complaint. A company with more than 100 items in its FTC file might not be bad at all. *Au contraire*, it might very well be a sterling outfit, proactive in the government's efforts to understand and regulate a particular industry. Read the items before drawing any conclusions.

polluting american communities

Scorecard.org
Environmental Defense Fund
HQ: New York City, New York

NO CHARGE   SEARCH

The Environmental Defense Fund packages information gathered by the government on pollution. For your own edification (or "nauseation"), type in the zip code of your residence, and Scorecard.org will tell you how polluted your surroundings are, and who rendered them so. I typed in my zip code and learned in seconds that I live in the bottom 20 percent of counties for air pollution, due almost entirely to a drug company, which is on my street, about a mile away—upwind. And so, for your sake, I am writing this as quickly as I can. To conduct research on a specific company, type in a name, and Scorecard.org will report all of its various emissions, one plant at a time. Not every company is bad, and the reports include scales that rank each plant against the rest of its respective industry, for cleanliness or smog-mongering.

scanning the media

Powerize.com
Corporate HQ: Linthicum,
Virginia

NO CHARGE   SEARCH

Powerize.com reads more than 10,000 publications, both print and online editions, and it can tell you in a second what has been written about any company, person, or subject. A free registration is required, and after that, you can log 10 different "alerts." The site will e-mail you whenever something is written about the company or subject in question. In the olden days, Powerize would have been a clipping service, sending envelopes full of newspaper articles, culled by people with the rather fun job of reading the paper with a pair of scissors in hand. There are other electronic clipping services, but Powerize.com is an excellent one, especially since it is among the few that do not charge a fee.

complete dossier

KnowX.com
Database Technologies
Corporate HQ: Atlanta, Georgia

NO CHARGE   SEARCH   E-COM

Database Technologies (DBT.com) can produce a complete background check on any person or company, drawing from both its own files and many others. It knows what you ate for breakfast and with whom—if not that, then nearly so. That is the sort of modern development that may very well make you want to move to a remote island where there aren't any databases, or, on the other hand, it might make you want to look up some person or company to get all the goods on them. As a matter of fact, neither alternative is possible. There are no islands without databases, this being the twenty-first century. As for looking someone else up, DBT.com is strictly limited to use by private investigators. However, the company has a second site, KnowX.com, where you can request searches of at least several dozen databases. Some of the searches are free,

but others carry charges of $1.50 to $15.00. Among the searches related to company research are bankruptcy, stock ownership, sales tax permits, and professional licenses.

credit worthiness

DnB.com
Dun & Bradstreet
Corporate HQ: Murray Hill, New Jersey

SEARCH   E-COM

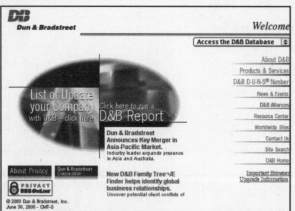

Most of the services included in this book are free, but D&B's company reports have been standard within the American business world for more than a 150 years, so they may merit your attention, and a few of your dollars. On the DnB.com homepage, press Products, and you will be able to select and order any one of about 15 reports, both statistical and analytical. The pricing is a bit trickier to find, partly because the rates vary, depending on the nationality of the company under review. This is all you have to do to find specific pricing, starting from the homepage: Move from About D&B to Contact Us, to In This Section—FAQ, to How Do I Become a Customer? to Order a D&B Report, to FAQ. About 23 questions from the top, "What is the cost?" is right there in plain sight. What could be simpler?

The bulwark of the D&B reports is the Business Information Report ($89), which includes general information and a credit history. Dividing it into roughly two sections, the company offers the Credit Scoring Report ($49), which describes the likelihood of a certain company paying its bills within 90 days, and the Background Report ($23), which offers only a description of the company and its recent history.

Yahoo! definition

Securities & Exchange Commission (SEC): The Securities & Exchange Commission oversees the trading part of the investment world, gathering data on entities issuing stocks, bonds, mutual funds, and so on, down a long list of vehicles defined as securities by the government. In addition to accepting legal filings, the SEC is charged with defending the interests of all those in the markets, starting with the individual investor.

Predominantly a links page as of this writing, BusinessHistory.net is attempting to generate original profiles, as well. The goal is admirable, since companies, however old they are, often depend on history to guide them in terms of their personality and reason for existence. We hope that the site continues to build its library of company lore and that it has a long future in history.

Company Research

* Develop an outline of information about any company in which you are considering investing.

* Make an active effort to relate news stories about a company which you follow to the information that you have already collected.

* If you have a company, periodically check the information that is filed publicly about it and correct errors.

* Much of the information discussed in this chapter is considered "fundamental research." Compare it to the technical analysis in the next chapter that approaches stock forecasting from a different perspective.

* Should you find anything disturbing about a company in the course of your fundamental research, as presented by the sites in this chapter, contact that company directly about it. If you own stock, contact the Investor Relations officer.

Technical analysis:
when everything's on the line

The stock market offers an endless prism of information, which technical analysis tries to sort into useful trends and indicators. As you learn about systems analysis, from the simplest to the most intricate, you will inevitably see into the mechanism behind the market and its moods.

Stock market analysis is really a matter of location: of finding the perfect perspective from which to observe the world of stocks, bonds, and funds. Presumably, some people are born with just the right viewpoint from which to spot the bargains, even if they can't explain how they do it. Technical analysts can always explain their choices. They look for consistency, not adventure, and they devote themselves to testing and honing different ways of assessing the market, circling ever closer to the great wellspring. Instead of divining rods, they have charts and systems, data, statistics, and historical precedent, and when they finally combine the right source material with the right formula, they will have achieved the great millennium: a perfect perspective on the investment market.

With the steps below, you can either latch onto a system that seems to make sense, or you can find the raw information with which to build your own technical analysis, and take it wherever you want to go.

Yahoo! definition

Chaikin's Oscillator: Developed by Marc Chaikin and others, the Chaikin Oscillator is a method of technical analysis that combines price and volume averages to generate stock trends.

Yahoo! definition

Moving Average: The average price of a stock during a designated time- span (such as one year) is traced on a chart known as a moving average. Averaging weeds out the spikes and shows the essential pattern.

step one: a stampede of systems
Sites that scout or provide formulas

In looking for the perfect recipe by which to distill the frenzy of the market into a few clear decisions, technical analysts often probe other systems as closely as they do their own. The first step in this section peruses systems and ideas, some of which may strike you as being worthy of a closer look. The first site, Equis.com, introduces a wide array of formulas, with commentary worthwhile for either new

Insiders' Tour of Yahoo!—Analysis

The stock quote service at the top of Yahoo! Finance (finance.yahoo.com) defaults to basic pricing for the most recent day's trading. However, if you scroll down the list of choices, past Basic to Detailed, you will receive a compilation of extensive financial data and news on any stock you specify.

TIP: The other quote service options (each of which presents trading information with a different emphasis) can be customized by clicking Edit; you will then have access to a wide array of available statistics. On the Detailed quote page for any stock, a small chart is included on the right side. By clicking Big chart just below it, you will not only enlarge the graphic, but also have the chance to manipulate the data: You can change the time span from the intraday up to five years. You can also set the chart up as a moving average, rather than a reading of the closing price.

TIP: The chart can be expanded to compare multiple stocks, or any stock to the performance of the Dow, Nasdaq or S&P average.

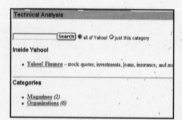

On the Yahoo! Finance main page, you will find two other resources which may be useful in technical analysis. Under Research, you can request historical quotes covering any timespan of approximately the past decade and under Reference, the Economic Calendar lists announcements scheduled for the current week, with forecasts of the expected statistics, if any. These general economic events can often, tied through analysis to stock performance.

or long-time students of technical analysis. BigCharts.com guides you through analysis, according to generally accepted priorities, while Sixer.com has ideas all its own.

The majority of websites that offer sophisticated analysis charge for the service. Most of them expect to see some money before you see any analysis. Quite a few offer a free trial, often limited to a few days or a couple of weeks. Equis.com is among the few that open at least a portion of their data to the curious public, at no charge. Happily enough, the pages that Equis offers free are what many full-service websites exact hefty fees for. Stock charts, listed under Free Stuff on the homepage, can be customized, using a long list of technical analysis formulas. Working in the other direction, from technical indicators backward to specific stocks, Equis.com offers 14 respective lists of Hot Stocks. You can also read daily commentaries regarding changes in indicators, those numbers or trends purported to illustrate the latest direction of the markets.

Technical analysis can be a formidable subject for the uninitiated. If it is true that some people don't understand a single word of it, then much of the expert commentary on the Internet, in the newspapers, and all over television, too, goes completely to waste. Should you ever come across anyone who doesn't know what a moving average is, let alone a Chaikin's Oscillator, send that person to the Equis tutorial called TAAZ (Technical Analysis from A to Z), based on a book of the same name by Stephen Achelis. It explains the many tools of the trade and includes a glossary of 80 oscillators (that is, 80 words).

Equis.com
Reuters
Corporate HQ: Salt Lake City, Utah

 NO CHARGE CALC. ARCHIVE

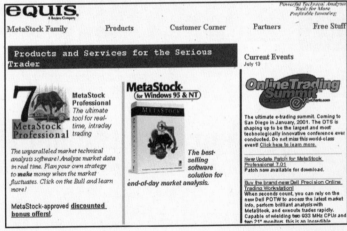

BigCharts.com is a subsidiary of MarketWatch.com, an all-purpose financial site best known for its affiliation with CBS. BigCharts concentrates on the abstracts that are indicated by its name, with a basic choice at the top of the homepage between Interactive charts or Quick charts. The interactive charts can be customized according to time-frame, indicator, and style, with a

BigCharts.com
Corporate HQ: Minneapolis, Minnesota

 NO CHARGE CALC.

further choice of stock comparison. Quick charts, which reflects a simple pricing history, requires only one: the name of a stock. The homepage also features market commentary from BigCharts cousin site, CBS.MarketWatch.com.

talk about technicals

Sixer.com
Corporate HQ: Arlington, Virginia

NO CHARGE   SEARCH

To many Americans, a "Sixer" is a professional basketball player for Philadelphia; however, to people from England who founded Sixer.com, it is a cricket term meaning something like a grand slam in baseball. The site keeps away from sticky wickets like fundamental analysis, which is the study of a company's fortunes within an industry, and concentrates on technical analysis, the study of its stock price within the market. Technical commentary regarding the day's events is featured in the middle of the homepage, along with a link to hour-by-hour Market Commentary from Briefing.com. (That is a bargain all by itself, since that site is otherwise a subscription service.) Sixer's own analytical method is to generate a list of under-performers, using certain algorithms, then narrowing that list according to other financial data. The method is explained and fully demonstrated on the site.

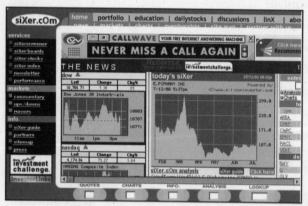

step two: technical analysis at work
How other people look into charts and statistics and pull out stocks

┌── Link List ──┐

Econ-Datalinks.org—American Statistical Association
StatPages.net—calculators by the hundreds for any type of analysis

The stock market seems to move on any number of axes, so it often seems, and so it can be proved. The range of priorities assigned by different analysts can be seen in the sites in Step Two. Zacks.com focuses on the nuances of corporate earnings reports, while UltraFS.com pinpoints those moments when the market is ripe for action. However these respective ideas mesh with your own, these sites show analysis as a form of investment philosophy that is, if nothing else, consistently applied.

Zacks.com

Corporate HQ: Chicago, Illinois

NO CHARGE   CALC.

Have you ever noted that billions of dollars are often gained or lost on the news of a mere penny's shift in a company's earnings-per-share report? The emotion leading up to an earnings report leaves more room for delight and disappointment than a junior high school dance. Like the belle of the ball, a popular company has to be very careful in the weeks leading up to the event, guiding suitors (brokerage house analysts) to a proper impression of the probable result—the reported earnings-per-share. If no one shepherds erroneous predictions in the right direction, upward or downward, then a fracas is bound to break out. When stocks either improve upon "street estimates" or fail to meet them, a trading fracas occurs immediately after the announcement. If one could only know in advance which reports were going to influence that fracas in trading, one could make a tidy profit—and that is the idea behind Zacks.com, which bases much of its technical analysis on out-predicting Wall Street's paid predictors (the analysts).

After lining up earnings-per-share (EPS) surprises to the best of its ability in advance, Zacks.com ranks stocks according to each company's ability to meet prevailing earnings estimates. About 316 stocks receive the highest rating for the probability of beating EPS estimates, and they are listed on the site. Zacks also offers access to commentary by about 40 technical analysts. Not all of it is updated every day, however. For stock-pickers wishing to bypass the analysis, the site also collects lists of stocks mentioned most frequently on brokerage "buy lists."

[At the time of this writing, the SEC was proposing a new regulation (coded "FD") to keep companies and analysts from being so furtive with earnings information; this regulation is by no means aimed at Zacks, though, which only operates within a previously existing situation.]

> ## Yahoo! Quote
> All the new financial products that have been created in recent years contribute economic value by unbundling risks and reallocating them in a highly calibrated manner. The rising share of finance in the business output of the United States and other countries is a measure of the economic value added by the ability of these new instruments and techniques to enhance the process of wealth creation. The reason, of course, is that information is critical to the evaluation of risk.
>
> —Alan Greenspan, "Technology & Financial Services" speech, April 14, 2000, www.bog.frb.fed.us/boarddocs/ speeches/2000/200000414.htm

timing the markets

UltraFS.com

Corporate HQ: Flower Mound, Texas

NO CHARGE E·COM

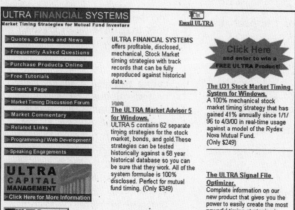

Question: what is the worst month, traditionally, for the stock market? Most people would say October. In truth, it is September (possibly because that is when all the pessimists suddenly realize that October is next). UltraFS.com charts such tendencies, believing that *when* you buy stocks may be more important, in the long run, than *what* you buy. While the site charges for the latest nuances of its research, it offers a free tutorial on the subject of market timing. Best of all, under the heading of Specific Stock Market Timing Systems, there is a lengthy list of entertaining facts: entertaining and well worth keeping in mind. In most years, for example, if you buy an average stock on the Monday before Thanksgiving and sell it on the third trading day in January, you would see a gain. Handy advice for buying stocks or amazing your friends.

step three: all you add is graph paper

The Internet provides all of the data that you need to experiment with your own formulas

Stock market analysis of any sorts feeds upon information, of course, and many of the sites in this section provide it in the form of raw numbers or charts. The sites in Step Three augment the current data available elsewhere, with indications of coming trends, at the Federal Reserve Board site, and historical data at NeatIdeas. No information is worth more than your ability to understand it, knowing where it came from, how it is constructed, and how it relates to other information.

gauging the business outlook

www.Federalreserve.gov/ fomc/beigebook/2000

The Federal Reserve Board HQ: Washington, D.C.

NO CHARGE ARCHIVE

Eight times a year, the Federal Reserve Board receives surveys on economic conditions from its regional boards, located all over the country. The reports, which cover the business outlook in the Reserve System's 12 regions, go into the Summary of Commentary on Current Economic Conditions, otherwise known as the Beige

Book. The Beige Book is intended to give a straightforward picture of the present and near future of the economy on a somewhat local level. The regional governors prepare their reports by talking to business people throughout their areas. Each report highlights only those topics relevant to the particular region, but they may include, for example, retail sales, wages, real estate, consumer spending, and construction. Though low on statistics, the Beige Book is very strong on trends, the very bowsprit of technical analysis, and the site may very well give you ideas for development.

Short Shots

HardRightEdge.com—daily commentary; also tutorials for beginners
TheStreet.com—briefings and analysis related to high-tech sectors

The full title of the NeatIdeas.com website is the Financial Forecast Center, and it certainly doesn't skimp on its soothsaying. Financial categories line both sides of the homepage, although no specific stocks are among the forecasts. It is hard to say exactly how the forecasts are generated, since the site is rather vague about the specifics of its applied reasoning. However, it is clear that, like most forecasts of future trends, it depends heavily on the past. NeatIdeas offers an extensive file of historical data, and I could not even count all the categories, though I tried, because each one leads to about a dozen more. In general terms, the site offers market data, as well as general economic numbers. The information on the Consumer Price Index goes back all the way to 1947. The exchange rates for various industrialized countries go back to about 1970. This is the sort of data that technical analysts use to test theories—just as though it were the present, rolling round and round for them on a wheel.

a mine for stock data

www.NeatIdeas.com
Applied Reasoning, Inc.
Corporate HQ: Decatur, Alabama

 NO CHARGE ARCHIVE

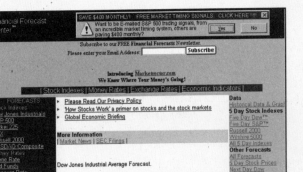

just one more thing . . .

Global Financial Data offers current economic and stock market numbers pertaining to 150 countries around the world, for sale by file (starting at $25) or on a subscription basis (at about $3,000 per year). However, all technical analysts are historians, as noted before, and the site is spectacular in providing them with free access to long-term data.

GlobalFinData.com
Corporate HQ: Los Angeles, California

 NO CHARGE ARCHIVE

Mind you, when GlobalFinData looks long term, it goes back to 1257. In case you weren't there, I'll note that 1257 was quite a good year to be long in silver, according to the Gold-Silver Ratio chart, which shows the years 1257-1999, inclusive. The inflation numbers go back almost as far, to 1264. Under "Stock Market Data," there is a cluster of charts noting the best and worst times to be in various world markets—starting with 1693. What, do you suppose, was the third-best day, on a percentage basis, that the U.S. markets have ever known? It was October 30, 1929, the very day after the famous crash. Let that be a lesson to you: One good bounce does not a Depression cure.

The Long and Short of — Technical Analysis

* Learn relatively simple systems first. (Some of the more accessible are the Arms Indicator, the Advance-Decline ratio and the Momentum Indicator.)

* Don't try to rush a trend: Be patient, and vow that you will not commit to a trade until the indications are exactly as you had planned or forecast.

* Technical analysis should not be the only basis for a trading decision. Good companies give any technical system the best chance of success.

* The Internet offers superb chart-drawing services, opening the art of analysis to everyone. To take advantage, you need to familiarize yourself with concepts behind the charts.

Futures and other specialized vehicles: beyond the stock answer

A number of investment vehicles take advantage of opportunities beyond the corporate and government economies, which are the basis of most stocks, bonds, and mutual funds. One of the most prominent, and volatile, are futures contracts based on commodities, or raw materials, such as wheat, gasoline, sugar, or silver.

Commodity futures are a great glory of modern economics. Developed in the nineteeth century, they have provided invaluable financial stability for those who actually produce or utilize commodities. The treacherous price swings that could put whole counties off the family farm overnight are a thing of the dim past. In the simplest sense, the futures market operates on the promise that traders make to deliver a certain amount of a commodity at a certain price and at a specific time. This promise is officially written as a contract, which can be bought and sold many times during the course of its standing.

The hundreds of commodity contracts in play at any one time turn risk into a very malleable element, where it was once as hard as rock. With futures, the risk associated with rising or falling prices is spread ever so thinly, among thousands of people or firms. That is the macroeconomic view. However, for individuals, the commodity futures market is nothing less than the roller derby of personal investing. At best, you will come home bruised in the ribs almost every night. At worst, you will get flung over the wall, never to return. This section is divided into just two steps: The first helps you to understand and perhaps trade in commodity futures, the second outlines three very different specialized vehicles popular among today's investors.

> **Yahoo! definition**
>
> **Contract:** The investment vehicle of the futures market, a contract provides for either the purchase or delivery of a set quantity of a commodity on a certain date.

The Use of the Futures Contract
Part A:
In Business

Before a farmer invests gobs of money and back-breaking effort in raising a new crop, he or she may want to establish that there will be a viable market for the final produce at harvest time. A futures contract can do just that, establishing a customer for the produce, or commodity, and setting a price. In many cases, there is no choice: A bank will often insist upon seeing a futures contract before it will lend a farmer the money with which to raise the crop. To give an example, a planter may contract to sell 5,000 bales of cotton next season at a good price. With that, the risk of losing a great deal of money in a falling or non-existent cotton market is reduced to nothing for the farmer. A textile company, on the other hand, may contract to buy those 5,000 bales, either to use the cotton or simply as a means of locking into a price on cotton. In the latter case, the textile company may sell the contract and use the money to buy other cotton better suited to its needs, but it will have used the futures market to ride the prices and defray the risk of a sudden upswing in prices. The use of the futures contract to offset risk in this and other ways is known as "hedging."

The Use of the Futures Contract
Part B:
In Speculation

Many people simply speculate on the price shifts of a contract, with no intention of using or supplying—or getting anywhere near—the underlying commodity, whether it is oil or wheat or cotton. In the introduction to this section, we warned that the futures market can be rugged. There are two reasons for that, and they intersect exactly on the fortunes of the futures speculator. First of all, commodities prices slide around quite a lot, relative to even the most volatile stocks. Weather, economic conditions, and global politics are just a few of the influences on markets, which really need no added influence, as they are notoriously skittish all by themselves. Second, futures contracts are purchased on a huge margin: A speculator puts up only about 10 percent of the total cost. In practice, a speculator who has leveraged a small amount into a hefty futures contract is jerked back and forth by that same leverage, in reverse. The price swings typical in commodities telescope down from the hefty contract and drive the original small stake that much more rigorously. The potential for such pronounced movement is the appeal, and the danger, of futures speculation.

step one: strap on padding

The Internet offers plenty of advice on futures, much of it questionable, with only a few sites with real information

Plain common sense is essential for the business of trading in commodities. First of all, one cannot be distracted by wishful thinking. To that end, the sites in this step do not treat the world of futures as a sweepstakes, in which you try to ride a number to easy money. Instead, they provide the clear-cut information that common sense requires. If you are new to futures, be sure to visit the first site, with advice from securities administrators. They have seen smarter people than you, who were bilked out of good money with promises of quick returns. Other sites in Step One will be of interest, whether you are already trading futures or still standing on the sideline.

protection from congames

One of the very hardest things to do in this world is to make money on a consistent basis in commodity futures. However, one of the easiest, it's sad to report, is to goad people into believing that they will make veritable fortunes on a consistent basis in futures. Those who do the goading are called "blue sky practitioners," because their promises are not worth anymore than so many feet of clear blue sky, according to the Kansas judge who first made their solicitations illegal in 1911. While that was a long time ago, the influence and ease of the Internet is allowing the practice to come into vogue with new impetus. The very first step for anyone considering a move into futures is to visit NASAA.org, for a look at Investor Education. There is a long list of congames and scurrilous schemes involving personal finance, but if you look specifically at Commodity Investments, you will see *Nine Questions to Ask Before Investing.* Ask 'em.

NASAA.org
North American Securities Administrators Association HQ: Washington, D.C.

NO CHARGE   ARCHIVE

data and basic information

TFC-Charts.w2d.com
Corporate HQ: Washington, D.C.

NO CHARGE

CALC.

The TFC-Charts website has extensive data regarding commodities, but it also offers a 12-step course in futures trading that introduces the basic process. Of course, it would take a 120-step course to fully prepare you, but the TFC "Short Course," as it's called, is a good start. The pride of the site lies in its charts, hence the name, TFC-Charts. You have a choice of 75 commodities, with pricing and other data drawn on a daily, weekly, or monthly basis, according to your preference. Keep in mind that the weekly chart is the only one that also includes computer-generated analysis on about two dozen points. TFC-Charts has an array of other pages, most of them original in content, since the site is attempting to be a free, full-service center for futures traders. Quotes are updated throughout the trading day.

close to the action

CRBindex.com
Commodity Research Bureau
Corporate HQ: Chicago, Illinois

NO CHARGE

Since its inception in 1933, the Commodity Research Bureau has tried to put the commodity trader nearer to the actual action at the exchanges: catching the rumors and impressions behind the prices. The website, CRBindex.com, generates a vast amount of editorial content, as it grants equal space and time to dozens of different commodities, from cocoa and coffee to oil and credit. In addition to daily news, the site offers the Bridge Trader, which takes a longer-range view with feature stories and in-depth analysis. It can be quite easy in the commodities futures whirl to buy a contract without quite knowing what it covers. Therefore, another practical part of CRBindex.com is a complete list of contract specifications, for every recognized commodity and country in the world

Futures.Net
Corporate HQ: Chicago, Illinois

NO CHARGE

Futures.net is a source for quotes and news in the commodities market. Of special note are its Pro-View Reports, which offer strong, independent comments on about eight of the major commodity groups, including energy and grains. Under Links, you can also find Market Snapshots, which draw on a variety of sources on the Internet to provide data on either general listings of commodities or on individual contracts, set according to a certain time.

Another site, Futuresweb.com, does nothing but collect linked data on futures; it is a good source for news, by itself, and a quick sampler of other sites, many of them devoted to a particular commodity or aspect of futures trading.

step two: cornering the corners of personal finance

The balanced portfolio sometimes looks beyond stocks, bonds, and mutual funds

Long ago, people didn't invest in very much aside from real estate and bags full of gold. Both are still essential to the civilized world and will always have worth, but they have been superseded as implements of capitalism. Small investors, in particular, tend to overlook them today. This step offers a potpourri of ideas built upon other types of investments, including gold and real estate, which offer particular strengths for the construction of your portfolio.

Gold.org
World Gold Council
HQ: London, England

NO CHARGE   ARCHIVE

According to the World Gold Council, a quarter of the gold taken out of the ground is put right back—stored in the basements of nations that use it as a reserve asset. If you are considering the wisdom of stashing some gold as a reserve asset, Gold.org has a downloadable booklet called "Investing in Gold," which will be of interest. The site, itself, has a weekly commentary on the gold market. At the time of this writing, the gold market had been so stable

for so long that a weekly comment is more than sufficient. Gold.org also carries information on activity that can affect gold pricing, including mining and industrial technology.

pricing gold

Kitco.com
Corporate HQ: Champlain, New York

NO CHARGE   QUOTES   E-COM

Kitco sells bullion, which is not the same as soup, but refers to any precious metal in its raw state, processed, purified, and ready for use. Bullion is usually sold in the form of bars, which Kitco sells in addition to coins struck in gold, silver, platinum, or other precious metals. The site lists daily closing prices, known as "fixings," in New York and London, for all of the above metals and also rhodium and palladium, which are becoming more prominent as investment commodities. The company does not comment on the markets, but is more practically positioned, offering instead an assay service (to test the purity of a precious metal) and information on subjects such as melting points, which are of interest to jewelry makers.

real estate for the small investor

NaREIT.com
HQ: Washington, D.C.

NO CHARGE

The institution known as a Real Estate Investment Trust (REIT, pronounced *reet*), allows the corporate doctrine to be applied to real estate investment; shareholders, some small, some quite large, pool funds in order to capitalize large ventures. The REIT was created through legislation in 1960, in order to encourage those massive building projects which seemed to be the answer to everything in the 1960s. Even so, REITs did not come into fashion in the financial world until the early 1990s, when investors noted with satisfaction that by statute, 95 percent of profits must be returned to shareholders every year. The REIT seemed to combine the opportunity for share-price gain with a very good chance of regular income. NaREIT.com describes the fundamental basics and lists some of the companies which operate as REITs. Most REITs, however, are traded on the major exchanges, and so a brokerage could also provide you with a complete list.

A hedge fund is officially a limited partnership in which you will buy into a company and share in its returns. That is the legal basis. In practical terms, it is a deluxe mutual fund, open only to those in the upperclass: "accredited investors" in the Securities & Exchange terminology. An accredited investor is one endowed with both financial experience and sizable assets, the idea being that these attributes will allay the disappointments that are always present with a risky vehicle. Another reason that hedge fund investors must be rich is that the funds are limited to only 100 partners; since the managers want to work with a sizable portfolio, they often set minimum investments of $1,000,000.

As any mutual fund manager will point out through gritted teeth, the hedge fund does not have nearly as many regulatory demands placed on it as a mutual fund. You should take note of that: While mutual funds must comply with rigorous (and very worthwhile) SEC filing rules, the hedge fund, as a limited partnership, makes most of its own rules. It can participate in activities closed to mutual funds, such as futures and short-selling. Be mighty careful, because in the fast lane of the hedge fund, you are on your own in many respects.

HedgeFund.net attempts to maintain complete information on hedge funds, which otherwise pride themselves on being fiercely independent of one another. You cannot look at the site's listing of 1,400 funds unless you qualify financially; basically, you must be a millionaire. However, HedgeFund.net offers considerable information, including the tracking of several of its own indices for hedge funds, even for those who do not choose to register (or don't qualify). The site also describes all the general types of hedge funds, which tend to mirror the major categories in mutual funds.

a complete resource

HedgeFund.net
Corporate HQ: Locust Valley,
New York

NO CHARGE

SEARCH

Short Shots

CFTC.gov—Commodity Futures Trading Commission
lgrub.com/visionquest—LimitUp futures simulator game
OptionsCentral.com—Options Industry Council, with downloadable booklet

Link List

FuturesLinks.net
www.netservers.com/~waldemar/list.shtml

just one more thing . . .

http://risk.ifci.ch
International Finance and
Commodities Institute
HQ: Geneva, Switzerland

NO CHARGE

ARCHIVE

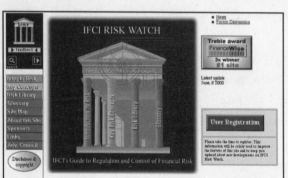

"The chain of events which led to the collapse of Barings, Britain's oldest merchant bank, is a demonstration of how *not* to manage a derivatives operation." That is the first sentence of Lillian Chew's study of the disastrous futures speculation that put Barings out of business after 200 years. Under the category Intro to Risk, the IFCI offers a handful of such Real Cases, in which a veritable hunger for unnecessary risk led to oblivion. Another study charts the 1998 collapse of the LTCM hedge fund, a report dotted with what the author calls "marker buoys": evidence of impending doom that was right out in the open, all the time. According to the International Finance and Commodities Institute, a trade group that is sponsored by large futures trading firms, the whole idea of risk management lies in spreading risk as thinly as possible. The site's Real Cases offer first-rate studies of what happens to those who accept that ever present temptation to take on more risk than necessary.

Futures and Other Specialized Vehicles

The Long and Short of

* The futures contract covers a wide range of commodities from wheat to credit to oil, specifying a price that must be honored on a certain date.

* Except under extraordinary circumstances, futures should not represent more than 10 to 15 percent of your investment portfolio.

* The option covers the right to buy or sell another investment vehicle, including stocks and futures contracts. It also specifies a price to be honored on a future trading date.

* Investors can participate in the real estate market through REITs, which trades through shares not unlike stocks.

* Hedge funds are investment pools organized as limited partnerships. They normally require a substantial minimum investment and operate under relatively few restrictions, compared to mutual funds.

Exchanges:
trading ideas

A publicly traded investment, such as a stock or a futures contract, finds a buyer through an exchange. The exchanges do not set prices, but oversee the trading methods that generate them, moment by moment. An understanding of these methods is vital to effective trading.

An exchange is not merely where a stock transaction is made, it is how it is made, as well. As the sites below describe, some stock prices are set through the open outcry of traders on the floor, shouting prices in an auction setting—or indicating them amid the din through hand signals. The automated quote system of Nasdaq, on the other hand, is utterly silent, depending only on the electronic transmission of bid-and-ask-information. Those who want to buy stocks (or sell them) with a set price in mind submit their bids-and-asks to computerized trading systems or to market makers, firms that literally deal in trades, buying and selling the same stock all day.

More and more, as individuals take responsibility for their own trading decisions, they will have an added choice in exactly how they want their investments traded, and where. Each site in this section represents either an exchange or other type of trading system. Each one can also provide good, hard-headed information about the products that it handles, from profiles of stock-issuing corporations to the weight information on a bushel of wheat (60 lbs).

step one: stock markets
The matchmakers that find buyers for sellers and vice versa

The stock exchanges in this country are private institutions upheld by public trust. They do not buy or sell stock; they only provide a venue (real or electronic) at which brokers and/or investors can circulate, trying to complete trades. Investors expect from them certain assurances of accurate accounting and trading practices, within

Insiders' Tour of Yahoo!—Exchanges

(finance.yahoo.com)

Look at Major U.S. Indices, for the current volume and composite averages on the NYSE and Nasdaq. These listings break down industry averages. From that page, go to the U.S. Market Digest for more about the day's trading, including new highs and lows and the number of issues that have advanced or declined.

TIP: **The Bulletin Board column in the U.S. Market Digest refers to lightly traded over-the-counter issues known as** *penny stocks.*

World Indices brings you benchmark indicators (equivalent to the Dow Jones Industrial Average) for every major exchange in the Americas, Asia, Europe, and elsewhere. There are also sections for news and charts regarding each exchange.

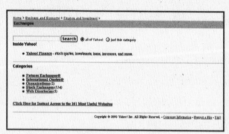

TIP: **Detailed coverage of international markets is also available on the international Yahoo! Finance. Links to all international sites are listed under World Finance at the bottom of the Yahoo! Finance page.**

NO CHARGE

Short Shots

NyBot.com—New York Board of Trade commodities market
Instinet.com—Reuters market maker, with new programs for individual investors

the practices of both listed companies and member firms (brokers allowed to transact shares). The sites in Step One represent the nation's major exchanges, and other options available for traders. Surveying the trading by the day and by the minute, these exchanges understand the process—and whatever your hot stock pick, money will also be gained or lost according to how well you grasp the process.

at the core of capitalism

NYSE.com
New York Stock Exchange
Corporate HQ: New York City, New York

NO CHARGE   SEARCH

For years, the New York Stock Exchange prided itself on its reputation as the trading center for shares in America's old established companies. The oldest, at least in terms of NYSE trading, is Con Edison, which has been listed on the exchange since 1824, when it was known as the New York Gas Light Company. However, now that trading excitement has shifted toward upstart companies and overseas stocks, the Listed Companies section of the NYSE website is boasting about the fact that two-thirds of the exchange's 3,085 companies were added only within the past 12 years. Using a world map on the site, you can see just how international the NYSE has become in that time. Clicking on a continent brings up a record of the listed companies for countries in that region—a globetrotter's stock screener—for anyone who wants to focus on Portuguese, Russian, or perhaps Malaysian securities. NYSE.com offers profiles and financial information for each of its listed stocks, along with current pricing and sales volume. In addition, you can create your own portfolio of up to 20 stocks, and the site will maintain it for you without charge.

center for news and quotes

NASDAQ.com
National Association of Securities Dealers Automated Quotation
Corporate HQ: Washington, D.C.

NO CHARGE   SEARCH   CALC.

There is only one thrill in watching a stock ticker . . . that moment when your stock goes by, of course. But what if every stock going by were one of your stocks, what if every day were Christmas? That is the sweet luxury of the Custom Stock Ticker offered on the Nasdaq site. You can designate stocks from any exchange or even mutual funds, and it will run a ticker just for you, with all the meaningful stocks and none of the fodder. The custom ticker will remain on your screen even after you've left Nasdaq.com.

Nasdaq was, itself, born with the computer age in securities trading, founded in 1971 as a fully automated system for the exchange of those fledgling securities known then as over-the-counter stocks. The faith it placed in the computer was richly returned, as the system grew apace with the thousands of high-tech

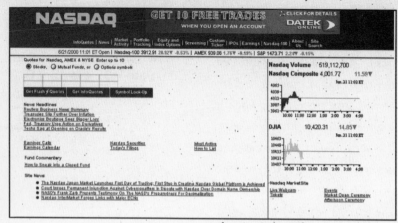

companies that found capital in equities markets and a place to trade on Nasdaq. One of the sheer fallacies left over from the over-the-counter days, however, is that just about any stock can be listed on the Nasdaq exchange: The website explains the accounting standards and trading regulations that govern listing. Overall, the site is heavily oriented toward news—about companies, general economic conditions, and about Nasdaq, of course. Sections devoted to earnings reports and initial public offerings sort news on those topics.

Now a subsidiary of Nasdaq, the American Stock Exchange, at Amex.com, has long been the kid brother among exchanges: No matter how old it got, it never quite grew up to the NYSE. Now it is giving itself a new identity, largely through new products such as index shares (which are described in the Mutual Funds section). The site provides details on the many changes underway at the American Stock Exchange.

on the fringes with small stocks

OTCBB.com

Corporate HQ: Washington, D.C.

NO CHARGE

SEARCH

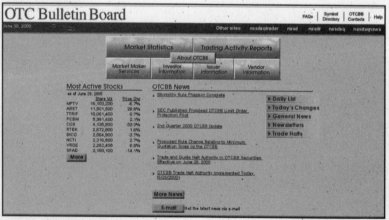

Nasdaq offers a specialized type of service at another site, OTCBB.com. The initials stand for "Over-the-Counter Bulletin Board," and the site delivers news and quotes about publicly traded companies that are not listed on any of the major exchanges. Such stocks are often known as penny stocks, operating under only basic Securities & Exchange Commission filing requirements and without the beneficial regulation of an exchange. If you feel compelled to trade penny stocks, you should take seriously the added risks for manipulation—or base mismanagement—that are always present in an obscure issue. OTCBB.com is providing some help for investors, simply by offering an objective quote and news service for a part of the investment world in which both of those commodities are especially scarce.

The latest development in exchanges is nothing less than the obviating of them. In a sense, Nasdaq led the way in the early 1970s, as its electronic transfer of bids and asking prices bypassed the open outcry of the trading floor. Now, ECNs, or "electronic communications networks," are allowing investors to trade directly with each other over the Internet. The trades are strictly anonymous, so it isn't as though you have to get chummy with anyone, but through ECNs, you do control your trading in real time. That is, there is no delay while a market-maker or exchange puts you on a list and then executes your order: You guide your trade toward its match, right before your eyes. The advantages over trades made through traditional exchanges lie in quicker execution, lower cost, and very possibly better prices on shares. The disadvantages are just as important: You have to work your trade yourself; there are typically steep account minimums, and, finally, only the most active shares receive enough action to optimize an ECN. It is hard to pick up shares in a sleepy company—or to unload them.

Tradescape.com offers access to a handful of ECNs, and its site explains the process very thoroughly, with illustrations and a glossary. For comparison, CyberCorp.com is another site offering investors a place in the ECN loop. BidnAsk.com also avoids exchanges in matching buyers and sellers. Please note that while none of these services are necessarily recommended, the modern investor should be up-to-date about this latest technique for trade-execution.

working your own trade

Tradescape.com
Corporate HQ: New York City, New York

E-COM

┌─ **Yahoo! definition** ─┐

Derivatives: Although corporate stock represents an actual share in a company, and a bushel of wheat is an actual, edible commodity, certain investments represent no such tangible goods or securities. They are only speculations on the future pricing of these various goods and securities, with value ultimately derived from that pricing. These vehicles, notably futures and options, are called *derivatives*.

step two: commodities markets

Commodities these days range from lean bacon to fat credit; for all of them, exchanges help predict the pace of change

It can be no coincidence that the two most aggressive commodities exchanges in America are located not far from each other in Chicago, straining for supremacy at every opportunity. For those cultivating a new interest in commodities futures, the Chicago Mercantile Exchange has information geared toward beginners. The Chicago Board of Exchange offers several very advanced tutorials on methods and strategies. As with any commodity exchange, current information is best for traded goods, and all of them have their specialties.

untangling the futures markets

CME.com
Chicago Mercantile Exchange
Corporate HQ: Chicago, Illinois

NO CHARGE   ARCHIVE

The Chicago Mercantile Exchange is one of the liveliest centers in the world for commodity futures trading, escorting contracts back and forth between investors, both through electronic trading and open outcry, as the noisy floor auctions are known. The website, CME.com, is one of the very best for education, including three online courses in futures and options, and two simulated trading games: one in futures and one in currency exchange. For those who are learning by doing, however, the site offers free real-time quotes in a selection of commodity contracts.

derivatives unlimited

CBOT.com
Chicago Board of Trade
HQ: Chicago, Illinois

NO CHARGE

The Chicago Board of Trade is another great commodity market in the Midwest. Especially inviting for analytical investors, this site has dozens of statistical databases available for downloading, ranging from the number of options exercised in a given timespan to the government's tally of weekly world rice production. In addition, the site offers commentary on market conditions, updated throughout the day and written by Board of Trade analysts on the spot in the trading pits.

In 1973, the CBOT introduced a new exchange devoted to equity options. Now it is a very large subsidiary called the Chicago Board of Options Exchange, handling about one-half of all the options trading in the country. Though options have been around for a long time, their full potential is not easily understood, and the website at CBOE.com is laden with educational features. Starting with The Basics, and leading through Strategy Discussions, it explores the veritable prism of complexities associated with the full use of options.

Yahoo! definition

Trading pits: At those exchanges where trades are conducted through live bidding, the trading floor is organized into centers, or "pits" that are devoted to the various products being traded.

The Nymex and associated Comex exchanges in New York City specialize in two types of products: energy fuels and precious metals. The website, Nymex.com, offers extensive prices on the dozens of specific commodities within each category. It is also a source of investor information, especially about precious metals, and specifically, about gold.

> **Special Note:** The United States has almost a dozen other commodities exchanges. Links to their sites and others around the world can be found through the links below.

Nymex.com
New York Mercantile Exchange
Corporate HQ: New York City, New York

NO CHARGE

step three: foreign exchanges
Capitalism in North America from Montreal to Mexico City

Due to new trade agreements including the North American Free Trade Agreement, many people consider a "domestic" portfolio to be one that includes stocks from Canada, the United States, or Mexico. For most American investors, Canadian and Mexican stocks are still best traded through U.S. exchanges, but the sites below can offer the best perspective on publicly-traded companies north of the 48th parallel or south of the Rio Grande.

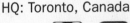

Link List

www.duke.edu/~charvey/links/finlinks.htm
www.interlog.com/~glenmanr/wjh/home1/html

From 1999 through 2000, the four major Canadian stock exchanges realigned themselves in the interest of competing less with each other and more with exchanges around the world. To that end, Toronto's exchange, at TSE.com, became the designated exchange for "senior" equities, ones issued by established companies. The Montreal Exchange, at ME.org, handles derivatives, such as futures and options, while Vancouver and Alberta, cooperating at VSE.com, are now each part of the Canadian Venture Exchange, for trade in the stock of newer companies.

BMV.com.mx is the website of the Bolsa Mexicana de Valores—the Mexican Stock Exchange. It is written in Spanish, but you can switch to the English version using a button at the top right of the homepage. The site is well organized, offering not only company profiles and current stock quotes, but links to the websites of listed companies that have them.

TSE.com
Toronto Stock Exchange
HQ: Toronto, Canada

NO CHARGE

SEARCH

BMV.com.mx
Mexican Stock Exchange
HQ: Mexico City, Mexico

NO CHARGE

SEARCH

WRHambrecht.com
W.R. Hambrecht & Co.

Corporate HQ: San Francisco, California

NO CHARGE   E-COM

If you ever wondered why you didn't get in on some high-flying IPO, and berated yourself for your sloth in forgetting to do so, here is good news: You probably wouldn't have gotten any shares anyway. In the typical Initial Public Offering (IPO), willing brokerages are assigned large blocks of shares to sell. If a new issue is even a little warm, then brokerages dole out the shares to their leading brokers, who bestow them upon their best clients. However, if the IPO is hot, then the brokerage may well keep some or all of the shares to trade for its own account. The average customer does not enjoy the spike when an IPO opens at three times its original price; the issuing corporation doesn't enjoy that spike, either, at least not directly. For these reasons, WRHambrecht.com developed Internet software that allows it to launch IPOs through an auction system designed to be fair to all concerned. If you like an upcoming IPO, based on the description on the site (or elsewhere), you can place a bid for a certain number of shares at a certain price. The number of shares you actually receive depends on the way the other bids fall, relative to yours. However, it doesn't depend on any of the following: how powerful you are, how rich you are, or with whom you played golf last Sunday.

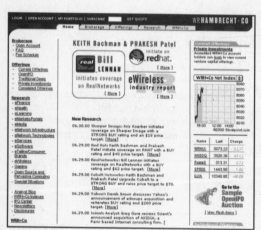

Consider Your Options
Part A:
The Impetus

Options were little known until the 1970s, when they were promoted by commodities exchanges looking for a product that would give them some piece of the excitement constantly surrounding stocks. Through an *option,* investors purchase the ability to buy or sell a particular product, usually a share of stock, on a certain future date and at a set price. If the going price is different on that date, then the option represents a profit or loss for the investor.

Options are similar to commodities futures, in that purchasers base decisions on their perceptions of future pricing. However, in larger economic terms, they are the hummingbirds, for they don't help support pricing against supply and demand, as do futures. What they do, by and large, is create a buzz around the stock market and give people another way to play in it. That isn't a bad thing, as long as people understand that the benefits of buying stocks are exactly the same as the drawbacks to buying options:

What is good about buying common stocks? You own a true piece of a company, a little piece of every stapler, contract, patent, and warehouse—and no one can take it away from you. Of course, the company can go out of business without a trace, but that is a very rare occurrence among companies listed on the major exchanges.

What is bad about buying options? You own nothing that is tangible or permanent, just the right to buy or sell stock on a certain date. When the date comes up, the option can be absolutely worthless. And that is not at all a rare occurrence.

An option example:

In the simplest instance, say you have purchased an option at $1 per share to buy the stock of Guppy, Inc. for $100 on January 1. If little fishes become a high-flying (so to speak) sector of the market and Guppy is going for $110 on that date, then the option is worth just about $10 per share: a profit of about $9 per share for you. If, however, big fishes move quickly into the market, and Guppy flounders down to $90 on January 1, then your option to buy it at $100 is worthless—you lose your $1 per share.

Options can anticipate a downward movement of stock. Let's say you purchase an option to sell Guppy, Inc. at $100 on January 1. It is not necessary to own any actual shares to sell on that date, you can sell or redeem your option through the exchange before that is necessary. Then, when the big fishes move in, and Guppy, Inc. goes down in price, you will be glad. On January 1, if Guppy is selling at $90 a share, you have a valuable option to sell it at $100. That option will be worth about $10. And again, referring to our example above, if Guppy goes up in price above $100, who would want the right to sell it down at $100? Your option would be worthless.

The right to buy shares at a certain price is a "call" option. Options to buy normally indicate a bullish attitude about the stock, meaning that you think it will go up. The right to sell shares at a set price is called a "put." That indicates a bearish stance, predicting that the stock will go down. To remember the terms, keep in mind that you *call* a bull (if you're a farmer), while you *put* as much distance as possible between yourself and a bear.

Consider Your Options
Part b:
The Strategies

People who own options are not necessarily investors. "Investor" is an honorable title, referring to people who place their money in support of an enterprise of business, government, or some other institution. Even if they are greedy finks, they are investors. Some of the people who buy options are investors. However, quite a number of them are simply speculators. A speculator is more akin to a bettor, putting money into an endeavor that can have no effect except the return of a profit (or loss). There isn't anything wrong with that, really, as long as that differentiation is maintained between an investor and a speculator.

Speculators buy options in the hope of receiving the benefits of stock movement, without committing the full price of the stock. The price of an option is typically only a couple of dollars; for that amount, you can ride the price changes of a stock that costs $50 or $100.

The price of the option is dependent upon two things:

In-the-Money or Out-of-the-Money: First, the option price is tied to the current stock price and where it sits relative to the "strike price," designated in the option itself. In the example introduced in Part A of "Consider Your Options," an option to buy Guppy, Inc. at $100 on January 1 was priced at $1. The strike price is $100. The current price of Guppy, let's say, is $90. It is "out-of-the-money," which means that the option could not be exercised at the present time, because nobody in their right mind would want the right to buy Guppy at $100, when they can pick it up on the open exchange at $90. As the current stock price draws closer to the strike price, the option goes up. For every dollar that Guppy goes above the strike price of $100, placing it "in-the-money," the option will go up a dollar, too.

Premium: Emotion is everywhere in the markets, and every option carries a popularity quotient known as the "premium." One stock that is 10 points out of the money may have an option price of 25 cents, while an identical option for another company, also 10 points out of the money, may cost $3.50. That is the premium, and it moves around with news and market mood. It typically decreases as the option expiration date (January 1 in our Guppy example) approaches.

Speculators buy and sell options without ever really owning anything at all. The chance of an option expiring worthlessly is very good, but there is a chance of doubling or tripling the seed money, too. Brokerages place strict income limits on those people interested in trading options, because at its worst, it is a form of gambling.

Investors use options, too. In a typical strategy, a person holding a number of shares in a stock such as Guppy, Inc., will also buy put options, covering the possibility of a sharp stock drop. Used in this manner, options are exactly the opposite of pell-mell speculation; they are a bulwark of conservative investment.

The Long and Short of Exchanges

* The New York Stock Exchange routes stock transactions through the live auction format of a trading floor.

* Nasdaq relies entirely on a computerized system and firms called "market makers," which involve themselves in the trading of designated stocks to ensure a responsive market under all conditions.

* Commodity exchanges execute trading in commodity futures. There are major commodity exchanges in Chicago, New York City and several other U.S. cities.

Education:

mind you

Everyone in the financial world knows that the whole endeavor of investing is based on absorbing information and somehow turning it into knowledge. The skills involved with that never-ending process can be learned, honed, and, in certain legendary cases, even perfected.

The shocking thing is that many people who are already investing heavily on their own counsel wouldn't even rank as beginners in the world of finance, which is like trying the high dive before knowing how to swim. Perhaps it doesn't matter in a booming market (it does!), but can a neophyte continue to make money in a down market? Does a neophyte know how to recognize a down market?

This section probably should have been first in the book instead of last, except that it is often hard to know how much you don't know, until you've been around the block once or twice. The sites below treat investor education from many points-of-view, dopey to dead-serious, because it is important for you to connect with the one that appeals to you. Nothing is taught, as they say, until it is learned.

Short Shots

InvestorWords.com—glossary of 5,000 terms
InvestorEducation.org—links to educational pages on other sites
sec.gov/oiea1.htm—U.S. government's Security Exchange Commission Office of Investor Education and Assistance
Investors.com—learning center

step one: beginners served here
Learning is a lifelong pursuit in finance

One of the intimidating aspects of investing is the sheer number of slang words and jargon that serve as shortcuts through the fogs of information choking the financial world. You might consider yourself bilingual if you can fully understand the average financial analyst's website column. Glossaries (such as InvestorWords.com) can teach the meaning of words, but the beginning sites listed in Step

Link List

http://miti@wallstreetnet.com
www.cob.ohio-state.edu/fin/journal/jofsites.htm

Insiders' Tour of Yahoo!—Education
(financevision.yahoo.com)

Yahoo! Finance's live broadcast, Y! FinanceVision, features interviews with informed guests throughout the trading day. Those watching the webcast can ask questions in real time, making FinanceVision a unique learning opportunity for novice or expert investors. FinanceVision has regular features, as well, which can be played at your convenience 24 hours a day. Feature topics include general subjects such as wealth, in which the site might focus on divorce, for example. In addition to original broadcast material, FinanceVision offers market data and news.

Another educational resource at Yahoo! Finance is the glossary (biz.yahoo.com/f/g/g.html), compiled by Duke University professor Campbell Harvey, which explains investment terms from Abandonment Option to Zscore. You can try your stock-picking skills without risking any money; in fact you might win some by participating in the Yahoo! Investment Challenge. You will start with an account of $100,000 and use it to trade a portfolio of NYSE, Amex, and Nasdaq stocks. Monthly winners receive cash prizes, and everyone has the chance to learn the markets at no cost at all.

One teach the language: its connotations, its values, and its emphases. All of them take it slow and easy, for the most unnecessarily intimidating thing of all about the language of investing is the maddening pace it too often evokes.

Vanguard's university, featured prominently on the homepage, consists of 10 courses, each of which is made up of one to two dozen "lessons." You can either take a whole course, or simply find a lesson you know that you need. The roster is weighted toward mutual funds, Vanguard's core business, and while some of the lessons inch toward sales talk near the end, the university is still one of the best investor education sites on the Internet for one simple reason: It is well edited and easy to read and understand. That makes quite a difference when someone is trying to absorb a lasting concept, and not merely bits and pieces. Under Education, Planning and Advice, the site also offers Plain Talk brochures on an even wider variety of topics than those covered by the courses.

plain talk

Vanguard.com
The Vanguard Group
Corporate HQ: Valley Forge, Pennsylvania

NO CHARGE   CALC.   E-COM

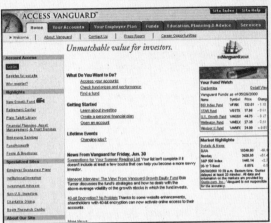

saving and investing

Library.thinkquest.org/10326
InvestSmart
Corporate HQ: Los Angeles, California

NO CHARGE

As part of an Internet competition sponsored by ThinkQuest, three high school students produced a site called InvestSmart in 1997 which has become a favorite with student investors. The first section is devoted to savings and emphasizes the futility of borrowing for anything except real necessities, and the value of compounding. Dr. Samuel Johnson, the eighteenth-century lexicographer, is the site's expert on saving, with his typically sensible admonition to spend less than you earn. The next section is lengthier and describes stocks, mutual funds, tax issues, and other central topics in personal finance. In real cases, two of the site's producers relate their own experiences as investors. The one named George demonstrates his youth and the fact that he has yet to experience anything but a bull market when he concludes his discussion of a certain mutual fund purchase by observing, "even if my fund returns only 15 percent a year, I will have doubled my $1,000 in six years." (All you kids out there, take heed: Someday, George will be glad when that same mutual fund *loses* only 15 percent a year.)

investors union

AAII.org
American Association of Individual Investors

Corporate HQ: Chicago, Illinois

CALC.

E-COM

About one-third of the material on AAII's advocacy site is free to guests; the more specialized information, however, requires membership, which costs $39 to $49. Since the organization has long defended the interests of private investors against the institutions that tower over Wall Street, a membership is something to be considered on its own merits. However, it will also open the door wide to the AAII's online tutorials, including those on planning, stock selection, and broker issues. In the ProPicks section, you can see how three Wall Street professionals invest $100,000. AAII is adamant about consumer advocacy, even where it is, itself, concerned: Not only can you take a free trial before becoming a member . . . you must take it. It's the rule.

step two: intermediates look around

You may be confident in one area of personal finance but lacking in another

a full syllabus

http://ws1.dju.com
Dow Jones University, Dow Jones & Co.

Corporate HQ: New York City, New York

E-COM

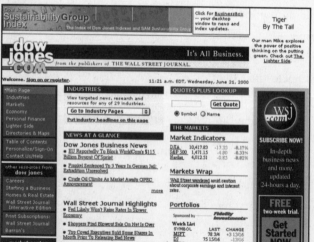

The most formal of the education sites listed in this section, Dow Jones University, actually has a faculty, course schedules, and tuition. The course list offers 10 different classes, ranging from an introduction to investing through bonds, options techniques, and a rather unexpected entry on Islamic investing. The courses are self-paced, composed of six lessons, taking an estimated 90 minutes each to complete. Nonetheless, there is an eight-week schedule for each "semester," partly to accommodate occasional class chats with the teacher. In addition, during the run of the course, students are accorded access to the Dow Jones and Barron's websites, which normally require a subscription. The cost of a course is $49 to $59, and those who pass the tests along the way receive a certificate. It may be hard to judge in advance just how much you know about a particular subject relative to the class work, and so the course list provides a short quiz for each offering. Your score ought to answer any idle wondering about whether you should take the course or volunteer to teach it next time.

short essays on specific topics

Investment-FAQ.com
Christopher Lott
Corporate HQ: Morristown, New Jersey

NO CHARGE

Over the years, Investment-FAQ (Frequently Asked Questions) has compiled a full library of articles, written in answer to typical inquiries about finance. The essays, contributed by investment professionals, are longer than mere definitions, yet they are succinct. You can either search by topic words or browse certain categories for enrichment, but there is no course organization on the site. Maintained by an individual named Christopher Lott, Investment-FAQ is intended to support other sites, as you are exploring them, ending confusion before it has a chance to settle in.

answers and questions

Morningstar.com/cover/ university
Morningstar, Inc.
Corporate HQ: Chicago, Illinois

NO CHARGE

Morningstar's "university" is more like a seminar than a lecture. Nearly all information is imparted in question-and-answer form, and visitors are encouraged to send in new questions. For example, one visitor recently asked about "do nothing" mutual-fund managers, whose work could just as easily be done by a child. The question was referring to managers of index funds, which are supposed to mirror the content and performance of one of the well-known stock indices, such as the S&P 500. The answers at Morningstar are indepth and often surprising. The response regarding the index fund managers explained how many decisions affect an index fund: For example, whether conditions of the moment make it more advantageous to buy the stock, when a purchase is necessary, or choosing a futures contract on the stock. Because of such decisions, actual performance on the exact type of index fund was shown to range between 8.8 percent to 10.8 percent in a given year. The level of the commentary on the Morningstar university page makes it quite a lot like a thought-provoking seminar, to be taken only after one of the survey courses in Step One.

step three: experts' fine tuning

Sites that challenge you to see the biggest possible picture with the littlest possible facts

The two sites in this step may well be of interest to investors of any level. They offer perspectives on investing that go beyond the mere making of money. Drawing from the science of economics, each treats the markets as a laboratory of behavior—some of it human, some herd-like, and some with the life spirit found wherever numbers congregate.

a lively look at the overall numbers

DismalScientist.com
Corporate HQ: West Chester, Pennsylvania

NO CHARGE

ARCHIVE

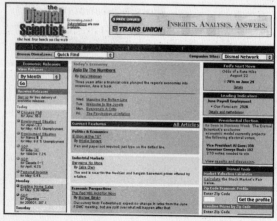

The name, DismalScientist, is a reference to economics, sometimes called "the dismal science." You can decide for yourself how that notion took hold, though the fact that commercial activity doesn't always unfold as predicted may have something to do with it, making economics occasionally an aggravating science, if not a downright dismal one. DismalScientist.com makes it a lively pursuit, nonetheless, with a pleasing mix of commentary and the latest statistical measures, from Mexican employment to oil and gas inventories. Each piece of such data says something very distinct about both the past and the future. That, in short, is the study of economics.

thought-provoking studies

www3.oup.co.uk/revfin/contents
Review of Financial Studies
Corporate HQ: Oxford, England

NO CHARGE

ARCHIVE

Though published in England, the *Review of Financial Studies* has a decidedly U.S. roster of contributors, most of them connected to the better business schools in the United States. The journal is entirely accessible online, with downloadable articles from either the current or past issues. The articles tend to concentrate on the activities of markets and traders: detailed viewpoints on the financial world, just as the way many individuals participate in it. One recent issue led off with an article on the advisability of a world market, followed by a piece containing a detailed discussion of trading volume. Though academic in style, which is to say unyielding to the casual reader, the *Review of Financial Studies* contains a level of detail rarely found in the trade press.

just one more thing . . .

HSX.com
Hollywood Stock Exchange
Corporate HQ: Los Angeles, California

NO CHARGE

The Hollywood Stock Exchange operates exactly like any other stock market, except that the securities underlying the stocks are not corporations, they are actors, actresses, directors, and movies. With the shifting fortunes brought by each day's entertainment news, the market reacts and prices go up or down. Shares in Anthony Hopkins, for example, were $1,650 when I last looked. There is even an active derivatives market, with trading in options. Of course, it is all fake money and has no real relation to any of the stars or the actual business of Hollywood, but it does have something to do with the basic business of Wall Street.

Within the metier of the movie industry, the idea of the Hollywood Stock Exchange is no doubt a glib one, since Hollywood stars are considered not much more than commodities, like pork bellies (some having more value than others, at that). For beginning investors, though, HSX.com separates the *processes* of finance from the financial world. I imagine that there are a great many people who could feel more comfortable learning about investing, if the underlying subject were more familiar to them. And better-looking, to boot.

Education

* After you understand the basic workings of the financial markets, choose one small area to study in greater depth. Your enthusiasm is bound to take root on that small beachhead and from there you can expand. In other words: Don't try to learn everything at once, and in equal measure.

* Choose one company for which you have a natural curiosity or affinity and make a study of it. With your increased familiarity with it, you will be able to decipher some of the otherwise abstract statistics bandied about in the stock world. You will find that learning to evaluate one company will help you to evaluate any company.

* Keep a glossary at hand (Yahoo! Finance offers a good one, as does Investor-Words.com). It is too easy to become confused and then bored when you don't understand the jargon in any field—and Wall Street happens to be riddled, quite literally, in fact, with jargon.

* Don't become too dependent for financial comment on any one publication or editorial website. Perusing other opinions on occasion will increase your education by exposing you to a variety of priorities and viewpoints.

* If you are in New York or Chicago, visit an exchange. Seeing the market at work will describe it for you better than any text. It will also fan your enthusiasm, which is probably why most exchanges have such nice visitors' galleries, in the first place.

Conclusion

Learning by doing isn't really the best way when it comes to certain activities: cliff-diving, as one example; cooking with wild mushrooms, as another—or finance.

But when it comes to finance, the Internet offers the chance to learn practically anything at all before you commit a dime. The cliffs, in other words, are not real until you are good and ready to jump. That is the dimension, inspired this book. It was never meant to tell you what to you what to do, but rather to see that you learn for yourself, using a couple of trillion dollars worth of educational material found lying around for free on the Internet. On the sites we've recommended, you can read if you like to read, but that isn't all. You can calculate, investigate, analyze and figure, if you prefer to be active. Best of all, you can practice with fake money that surely seems real, and make blunders which, happily enough, do not. With the sites covered in this book, you can see just what the experts do, in terms of news and research. If fact, with our book before you and the whole Internet beyond, you are an expert, to whatever extent you want to be.

pecial thanks

The author would like to thank her brother, David, and sister-in-law, Terriruth: internet pioneers, both. Paul Birchmeyer is an authority on auctions, online or off, his influence was always welcome. The author would also like to thank the book's editor, Dinah Dunn, for making all of the work fun (even when it probably wasn't, come to think of it) and for great ideas along the way; Byron Preiss, Kelly Smith, and Jeanine Campbell at BPVP; Megan Newman and Matthew Benjamin at HarperCollins; Angela Screbant and Jami Heldt at Yahoo! Inc.; John Leonhardt at Panic Entertainment. As always, there is Neddy, too.

Site index

Please note that all the entries in this book are prefaced with http://. Also note that many sites have dropped the www. prefix, while other still require it. Be sure to try the URL with and without the www. when having difficulty finding any of the sites listed below.

Subject index